Growth and Interaction in the World Economy

The Roots of Modernity

Angus Maddison

The AEI Press

Publisher for the American Enterprise Institute

WASHINGTON, D.C.

Available in the United States from the AEI Press, c/o Client Distribution Services, 193 Edwards Drive, Jackson, TN 38301. To order, call toll free: 1-800-343-4499. Distributed outside the United States by arrangement with Eurospan, 3 Henrietta Street, London WC2E 8LU, England.

Library of Congress Cataloging-in-Publication Data

Maddison, Angus
    Growth and interaction in the world economy: the roots of modernity/ Angus Maddison.
        p. cm.
    Includes bibliographical references.
    ISBN 0-8447-7173-2 (pbk. : alk. paper)
    1. Economic history—16th century. 2. Economic history—1600–1750. 3. Economic history—1750–1918. 4. International economic relations I. Title.

HC51.M266 2004
330.9'03—dc22

                                                    2003063873

10 09 08 07 06 05 04   1 2 3 4 5

Printed in the United States of America

THE HENRY WENDT LECTURE SERIES

The Henry Wendt Lecture is delivered annually at the American Enterprise Institute by a scholar who has made major contributions to our understanding of the modern phenomenon of globalization and its consequences for social welfare, government policy, and the expansion of liberal political institutions. The lecture series is part of AEI's Wendt Program in Global Political Economy, established through the generosity of the SmithKline Beecham pharmaceutical company (now GlaxoSmithKline) and Mr. Henry Wendt, former chairman and chief executive officer of SmithKline Beecham and trustee emeritus of AEI.

GROWTH AND INTERACTION IN THE WORLD ECONOMY:
THE ROOTS OF MODERNITY
Angus Maddison, 2001

IN DEFENSE OF EMPIRES
Deepak Lal, 2002

THE POLITICAL ECONOMY OF WORLD MASS MIGRATION:
COMPARING TWO GLOBAL CENTURIES
Jeffrey G. Williamson, 2004

Contents

Illustrations

vii

Introduction

The main objectives of this essay are to explain why the West got rich, when its ascension began, how its economic development diverged from that in the rest of the world, and the nature of the interaction between the "West" (Western Europe, the United States, Canada, Australia, New Zealand, and Japan) and the "Rest" of the world.

Since 1820, modern economic growth has been very rapid by historical standards, and quantitative indicators have been relatively abundant. To go back earlier involves use of weaker evidence and greater reliance on clues and conjecture. Nevertheless, it is worth the effort because differences in the pace and pattern of change have deep roots in the past, and there is substantial disagreement on the contours, causes, and timing of development in the West and the Rest.

There are two widely held interpretations that I think are wrong:

a) the view that the world was caught in a "Malthusian trap," with living standards oscillating around subsistence levels for millennia because of technological stagnation and that deliverance came from a sudden takeoff, an "industrial revolution," originating in Lancashire in the last quarter of the eighteenth century;[1]

This essay is an extension of the Wendt lecture I gave at the American Enterprise Institute on May 15, 2001. I am grateful for comments I received during my stay at AEI and comments on a later version at a workshop at Harvard University in May 2002, organized by Armand Clesse of the Luxembourg Institute for European and International Studies.

1

b) the view that income levels in Asia and Europe were similar around 1800 and that divergence in their income levels emerged only within the past two centuries.[2]

Western ascension was not a sudden takeoff but a very lengthy process, with average per capita income rising nearly threefold from 1000 to 1820 compared with a rise of a third in the Rest. Eleventh century income *levels* were lower in the West than the Rest. By 1820, they were twice as high. Europe overtook Chinese levels in the fourteenth century. Between 1000 and 1820, population grew fivefold in the West, somewhat less than fourfold in the Rest. Both parts of the world experienced *extensive* as well as some degree of *intensive* growth. Neither part was caught in a Malthusian trap.

Technical progress was a slow crawl before the nineteenth century but had a major impact on the world economy. Dramatic progress in Western shipping and navigation permitted a twentyfold increase in world trade between 1500 and 1820. This brought gains from specialization of the type stressed by Adam Smith. It provided European consumers with new products: tea, coffee, cacao, sugar, tobacco, porcelain, silk, and cotton textiles. In relative terms, this globalization process was more important from 1500 to 1820 than in 1820–2001 (see table 6 on page 22).

Improvements in shipping and navigation (which were in large part the fruit of scientific endeavor) also led to the conquest and transformation of the Americas. World production potential was increased by an ecological transfer of plants and livestock across the Atlantic. The relative impact of this "Columbian exchange" was greatest in the Americas, which acquired cattle, pigs, chickens, sheep, goats, wheat, rice, sugar cane, coffee, vegetables, and fruits to enrich the diet, as well as horses and mules for transport and traction. There was a reciprocal transfer of New World crops to Europe, Asia, and Africa—maize, potatoes, sweet potatoes, manioc, tomatoes, peanuts, beans, pineapples, cocoa, and tobacco—which enhanced the rest of the world's capacity to sustain population growth.

There was also a diffusion of existing technologies between continents. Here, the biggest impact was felt in the stone-age economy of the Americas, which had not known metal tools, wheeled vehicles and ploughs, paper, or printing.

Part I provides a detailed history of these innovations and the other reasons for Western ascension before 1820. The treatment of later performance is much more cursory, as its nature is less subject to controversy and the major purpose of this essay is to explore the roots of modernity in the centuries before 1820. Parts II–IV analyze the interaction between the West and the economies of the Americas, Asia, and Africa and demonstrate the unique character of Western performance.

My judgment of the nature of long-run Western performance and its exceptional character does not differ greatly from that in Adam Smith (1776), David Landes (1998), or McNeill and McNeill (2003). What is new in my approach is systematic use of quantitative evidence in a macroeconomic framework.

Quantitative analysis of a macroeconomic kind can provide guidance on the broad contours of development and is a very useful complement to qualitative analysis. It can identify changes in the timing and scope of change that the qualitative approach, on its own, may leave fuzzy. It is easily contestable and likely to be contested. It can sharpen scholarly discussion on the causality of change, provoke a closer scrutiny of the evidence, and contribute to the dynamics of the research process.[3]

PART I

Why and When Did the West Get Rich?

Changes in the Momentum of Growth
over the Long Term

Over the past millennium, world population rose 23-fold, per-capita income 14-fold, and GDP more than 300-fold. This contrasts sharply with the preceding millennium, when world population grew by only a sixth, with no advance in per-capita income. From 1000 to 1820, growth was predominantly extensive. Most of the GDP increase went to accommodate a fourfold increase in population. The advance in per-capita income was a slow crawl—the world average increased only by half over a period of eight centuries.

In the year 1000, the average infant could expect to live about twenty-four years (see table 1). A third would die in the first year of life. Hunger and epidemic disease would ravage the survivors. By 1820, life expectancy had risen to thirty-six years in the West, with no improvement elsewhere.

After 1820, world development became much more dynamic. By 2001, income per head had risen ninefold, population nearly sixfold. Per-capita income rose by 1.2 percent a year, twenty-four times as fast as in 1000–1820. Population grew about 1 percent a year, six times as fast as in 1000–1820. Life expectancy increased to seventy-nine years in the West and sixty-four in the rest of the world.

Within the capitalist epoch (the period from 1820 onward), the pace of advance has been uneven. One can distinguish five distinct phases:

TABLE 1
LIFE EXPECTANCY, 1000–2002
(years at birth for both sexes combined)

	World	West	Rest
1000	24	24	24
1820	26	36	24
1900	31	46	26
1950	49	66	44
2002	66	79	64

SOURCE: Maddison (2001, 31), updated.

1. The "golden age," 1950–73, when world per capita income grew nearly 3 percent a year, was by far the best.

2. Our age, from 1973 onward (henceforth characterized as the neo-liberal order), is second best.

3. The old "liberal order" (1870–1913) was third best, only marginally slower in terms of per capita income growth.

4. In 1913–50, growth was well below potential because of two world wars and the intervening collapse of world trade, capital markets, and migration.

5. The slowest growth was registered in the initial phase of capitalist development (1820–70), when significant growth momentum was largely confined to European countries, Western offshoots, and Latin America.

The Divergence between the "West" and the "Rest"

The first panel of table 2 shows the evolution of per-capita income in seven major regions from 1000 to 2001. In the year 1000, the interregional spread was very narrow, a range of $400 to $450, measured in 1990 dollars. By 2001, all regions had increased their incomes, but there was an 18:1 gap between the richest and the poorest region and a much wider intercountry spread.

TABLE 2

LEVELS OF PER-CAPITA GDP, POPULATION, AND GDP:
WORLD AND MAJOR REGIONS, 1000–2001

	1000	1500	1820	1870	1913	1950	1973	2001
Levels of per-capita GDP (1990 international dollars)								
Western Europe	400	771	1,204	1,960	3,458	4,579	11,416	19,256
Western offshoots	400	400	1,202	2,419	5,233	9,268	16,179	26,943
Japan	425	500	669	737	1,387	1,921	11,434	20,683
West	405	702	1,109	1,882	3,672	5,649	13,082	22,509
Asia (excluding Japan)	450	572	577	550	658	634	1,226	3,256
Latin America	400	416	692	681	1,481	2,506	4,504	5,811
E. Europe & f. USSR	400	498	686	941	1,558	2,602	5,731	5,038
Africa	425	414	420	500	637	894	1,410	1,489
Rest	441	538	578	606	860	1,091	2,072	3,372
World	436	566	667	875	1,525	2,111	4,091	6,049
Interregional spread	1.1:1	1.9:1	2.9:1	4.8:1	8.2:1	14.6:1	13.2:1	18.1:1
West/Rest spread	0.9:1	1.3:1	1.9:1	3.1:1	4.3:1	5.2:1	6.3:1	6.7:1
Population (millions)								
Western Europe	25	57	133	188	261	305	358	392
Western offshoots	2	3	11	46	111	176	251	340
Japan	8	15	31	34	52	84	109	127
West	35	75	175	268	424	565	718	859
Asia (excluding Japan)	175	268	679	731	926	1,299	2,140	3,527
Latin America	11	18	22	40	81	166	308	531
E. Europe & f. USSR	14	30	91	142	236	267	360	411
Africa	32	47	74	90	125	227	390	821
Rest	233	363	867	1,004	1,367	1,959	3,198	5,290
World	268	438	1,042	1,272	1,791	2,524	3,916	6,149
West/world (%)	13.0	17.2	16.8	21.1	23.7	22.4	18.3	14.0
Levels of GDP (millions of 1990 international dollars)								
Western Europe	10.2	44.2	160.1	367.6	902.3	1,396	4,096	7,550
Western offshoots	0.8	1.1	13.5	111.5	582.9	1,635	4,058	9,156
Japan	3.2	7.7	20.7	25.4	71.7	161	1,243	2,625
West	14.1	53.0	194.4	504.5	1,556.9	3,193	9,398	19,331
Asia (excluding Japan)	78.9	153.6	392.2	401.6	608.7	823	2,623	11,481
Latin America	4.6	7.3	15.0	27.5	119.9	416	1,389	3,087
E. Europe & f. USSR	5.4	15.2	62.6	133.8	367.1	695	2,064	2,072
Africa	13.7	19.3	31.2	45.2	79.5	203	550	1,222
Rest	102.7	195.3	501.0	608.2	1,175.2	2,137	6,626	17,862
World	116.8	248.3	695.3	1,112.7	2,732.1	5,330	16,024	37,194
West/world (%)	12.1	21.3	28.0	45.3	57.0	59.9	58.6	52.0

SOURCE: Maddison (2003a, 256–62).

One can also see the divergence between the West and the Rest. Real per-capita income of the West increased nearly threefold between 1000 and 1820 and twentyfold from 1820 to 2001. In the rest of the world, income rose much more slowly, by a third from 1000 to 1820 and sixfold since then. The West had 52 percent of the world GDP in 2001, but only 14 percent of world population. Average income was about $22,500 (in 1990 purchasing power). The Rest, by contrast, with 86 percent of world population, had an average income of less than $3,400.

The Western Europe–China Dichotomy. The most solidly documented evidence on the long-term evolution of income levels relates to Western Europe and China. Two thousand years ago, these were the two most-advanced areas in terms of technology and institutions of governance. Income levels were probably similar until the fifth century, when the Western half of the Roman Empire collapsed under barbarian invasion. Its decline was reinforced in the seventh century by the Arab capture of Spain, North Africa, and most of Western Asia, which ended Western European commerce in the Mediterranean. There was no comparable collapse in China.

From the second half of the tenth century until late in the thirteenth, there was significant progress in China. The Sung dynasty successfully promoted intensive rice agriculture, and the center of gravity of population moved from North China to the area south of the Yangtze. From 1300 to 1850, population grew faster than in Western Europe, but per-capita income stagnated. The century after 1850 was disastrous. Civil wars and foreign invasions reduced per capita income by more than a quarter (see figure 1).

Western Europe's economic ascension began about the year 1000, continued to 1820, and accelerated thereafter. Western Europe caught up with Chinese income levels in the fourteenth century. By 1950, European per capita levels were ten times higher than the Chinese levels. The experience of China in the past half century, and particularly since the 1978 economic reform, shows clearly that divergence is not inexorable. China's economic resurrection has involved a very significant element of catch-up.

FIGURE 1
COMPARATIVE LEVELS OF GDP PER CAPITA:
CHINA AND WEST EUROPE, 400–2001
(in 1990 international dollars)

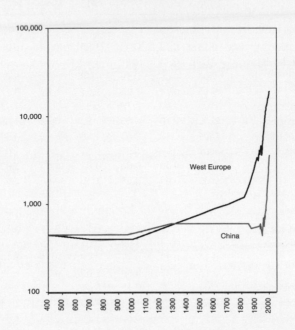

SOURCE: Maddison (1998, 2001, and 2003a).

Experience of Growth, Divergence, and Convergence since 1950.

In the past half-century, there have been major changes in the pace and pattern of growth in different parts of the world.

The years 1950 to 1973 were a golden age of unparalleled prosperity. World per capita GDP rose at an annual rate near 3 percent; world GDP, nearly 5 percent (see table 3); and exports almost 8 percent. Performance was better in all regions than in any earlier phase. There was a significant degree of convergence in per capita income and productivity, with most regions growing faster than the United States (the lead economy, with the highest productivity level).

TABLE 3

GROWTH RATES OF PER-CAPITA GDP, POPULATION, AND GDP, 1000–2001

(annual average compound growth rates)

	1000–1500	1500–1820	1820–1870	1870–1913	1913–1950	1950–1973	1973–2001
A. Per-capita GDP							
Western Europe	0.13	0.14	0.98	1.33	0.76	4.05	1.88
Western offshoots	0.00	0.34	1.41	1.81	1.56	2.45	1.84
Japan	0.03	0.09	0.19	1.48	0.88	8.06	2.14
West	**0.13**	**0.14**	**1.06**	**1.57**	**1.17**	**3.72**	**1.95**
Asia (excluding Japan)	0.05	0.00	–0.10	0.42	–0.10	2.91	3.55
Latin America	0.01	0.16	-0.03	1.82	1.43	2.58	0.91
E. Europe & f. USSR	0.04	0.10	0.63	1.18	1.40	3.49	–0.05
Africa	–0.01	0.00	0.35	0.57	0.92	2.00	0.19
Rest	**0.04**	**0.02**	**0.06**	**0.82**	**0.65**	**2.83**	**1.75**
World	**0.05**	**0.05**	**0.54**	**1.30**	**0.88**	**2.92**	**1.41**
B. Population							
Western Europe	0.16	0.26	0.69	0.77	0.42	0.71	0.32
Western offshoots	0.07	0.44	2.86	2.07	1.25	1.54	1.09
Japan	0.14	0.22	0.21	0.95	1.32	1.14	0.55
West	**0.15**	**0.27**	**0.86**	**1.07**	**0.78**	**1.05**	**0.64**
Asia (excluding Japan)	0.09	0.29	0.15	0.55	0.92	2.19	1.80
Latin America	0.09	0.07	1.25	1.63	1.96	2.73	1.96
E. Europe & f. USSR	0.15	0.35	0.89	1.19	0.33	1.31	0.47
Africa	0.07	0.15	0.40	0.75	1.64	2.37	2.69
Rest	**0.09**	**0.27**	**0.29**	**0.72**	**0.98**	**2.15**	**1.82**
World	**0.10**	**0.27**	**0.40**	**0.80**	**0.93**	**1.93**	**1.62**
C. GDP							
Western Europe	0.29	0.40	1.68	2.11	1.19	4.79	2.21
Western offshoots	0.07	0.78	4.31	3.92	2.83	4.03	2.95
Japan	0.18	0.31	0.41	2.44	2.21	9.29	2.71
West	**0.27**	**0.41**	**1.93**	**2.66**	**1.96**	**4.81**	**2.61**
Asia (excluding Japan)	0.13	0.29	0.05	0.97	0.82	5.17	5.41
Latin America	0.09	0.23	1.22	3.48	3.42	5.38	2.89
E. Europe & f. USSR	0.21	0.44	1.53	2.37	1.74	4.85	0.01
Africa	0.07	0.15	0.75	1.32	2.57	4.43	2.89
Rest	**0.13**	**0.29**	**0.39**	**1.54**	**1.63**	**5.04**	**3.61**
World	**0.15**	**0.32**	**0.93**	**2.11**	**1.82**	**4.90**	**3.05**

SOURCE: Maddison (2003a, 257–63).

After 1973, there was a marked slowdown in world growth. There was substantial divergence between different regions, and performance in many of them was below potential.

In the advanced capitalist countries, per capita GDP growth slowed substantially after 1973. To a significant degree, this was due to a deceleration of technical progress in the United States, the country operating closest to the frontier of technology. There was less scope for rapid catch-up in productivity in Western Europe and Japan, as these "follower" countries (i.e., those lagging behind the United States) had eroded the once-and-for-all opportunities they exploited in the golden age. Some slowdown in these economies was warranted, but policy failings made it bigger than it need have been (see Maddison 2001, 131–41 for a detailed analysis).

By far the best performance in 1973–2001 came from fifteen economies of East Asia, which produce a quarter of world GDP and have half the world's population. The success of resurgent Asia has been extraordinary. Per capita growth was faster after 1973 than in the golden age and more than ten times as fast as in the old liberal order (1870–1913). There has been significant catch-up on the advanced capitalist group and a replication (in various degrees of intensity) of the big leap forward achieved by Japan in the golden age.

If the world consisted only of the advanced capitalist countries and resurgent Asia, the pattern of development since 1973 could be interpreted as a clear demonstration of the possibilities for conditional convergence suggested by neoclassic growth theory. This supposes that countries with low incomes have "opportunities of backwardness" and should be able to attain faster growth than more prosperous economies operating nearer the technological frontier. This potential can be realized only if such countries are successful in mobilizing and allocating resources efficiently, improving their human and physical capital to assimilate and adapt appropriate technologies. The resurgent Asian countries were successful in seizing these opportunities.

All other regions of the world did very badly in 1973–2001. The loss of momentum was very sharp in Africa, Latin America, and the

Middle East. These economies suffered major shocks as the result of the slowdown in the advanced capitalist countries. The shocks crippled their growth momentum and left their economic policy in disarray. Their economic performance in the golden age had not been due to any great virtues of domestic policy but was dependent on the diffusion effects of high growth momentum in the advanced countries. The sharp slowdown in the capitalist core sparked off debt crises, inflation, and fiscal and monetary problems in Latin America and Africa. In the Middle East, fluctuating oil prices and wars affecting Iran, Iraq, and Lebanon were major disturbing forces. The biggest of these system shocks was the political and economic collapse that accompanied the disintegration of the USSR into fifteen independent states. This shock also led to political change in East European countries and the collapse of their command economies. These successor states of the USSR had major problems in adjusting their policies and institutions in order to function successfully as new members of a capitalist world economy, which offered new opportunities for trade and access to foreign capital but also involved new dangers of instability and new rules of behavior.

The Driving Forces That Explain the Acceleration of Western Growth since 1820

In analyzing growth causality, it is useful to distinguish between proximate and measurable influences and deeper, nonquantifiable features that help explain the unique dynamism of Western European performance over several centuries.

For the period since 1820, it is possible to quantify the proximate causes that explain the performance of major capitalist economies (see the detailed accounts for the United Kingdom, United States, and Japan in table 4).

The United Kingdom was the lead country in terms of labor productivity in the nineteenth century and played a strongly diffusionist role in world development through export of capital and its policy of

TABLE 4

DETERMINANTS OF GROWTH: UK, USA, AND JAPAN, 1820–1998

	UK	USA	Japan	UK	USA	Japan
	Gross stock of machinery and equipment per capita (1990 $)			Gross stock of nonresidential structures per capita (1990 $)		
1820	92	87	n.a.	1,074	1,094	n.a.
1870	334	489	94[a]	2,509	3,686	593[a]
1913	878	2,749	329	3,215	14,696	852
1950	2,122	6,110	1,381	3,412	17,211	1,929
1973	6,203	10,762	6,431	9,585	24,366	12,778
1998	11,953	25,153	29,987	21,066	35,810	49,042
	Primary energy consumption per capita (tons of oil equiv.)			Average years of education[c] per person employed		
1820	.61	2.45[b]	0.20	2.00	1.75	1.50
1870	2.21	2.45	0.20	4.44	3.92	1.50
1913	3.24	4.47	0.42	8.82	7.86	5.36
1950	3.14	5.68	0.54	10.60	11.27	9.11
1973	3.93	8.19	2.98	11.66	14.58	12.09
1998	3.89	8.15	4.04	15.10	19.46	16.03
	Land area per capita (hectares)			Exports per capita (1990 $)		
1820	1.48	48.1	1.23	53	25	0
1870	1.00	23.4	1.11	390	62	2
1913	0.69	9.6	0.74	862	197	33
1950	0.48	6.2	0.44	781	283	42
1973	0.43	4.4	0.35	1,684	824	875
1998	0.41	3.5	0.30	4,680	2,755	2,736
	Hours worked per head of population			GDP per work hour (1990 $)		
1820	1,153	968	1,598	1.49	1.30	0.42
1870	1,251	1,084	1,598	2.55	2.25	0.46
1913	1,181	1,036	1,290	4.31	5.12	1.08
1950	904	756	925	7.93	12.65	2.08
1973	750	704	988	15.97	23.72	11.57
1998	657	791	905	27.45	34.55	22.54

SOURCE: Maddison (1995a, 252–55), augmented and updated.
NOTE: a. 1890. b. 1850. c. In equivalent years of primary education.

free trade. The United States overtook the United Kingdom as the productivity leader in the 1890s and had faster productivity growth thereafter. Japan was the archetype catch-up country, overtaking Chinese levels of performance in the Tokugawa period, catching up with Western Europe in terms of per capita GDP (but not productivity) by the 1990s. The Japanese catch-up effort involved high rates of investment in human and physical capital (which is also characteristic of other Asian economies—Korea, Taiwan, China, Hong Kong, and Singapore—where there has been substantial catch-up in the past half century). Instead of overtaking the United States, as was once predicted, the Japanese economy has stagnated in the past decade.

The most dynamic feature of the three countries was the explosive growth in the stock of machinery and equipment per head. It rose by a multiple of 130 in the United Kingdom and 289 in the United States between 1820 and 1998, and 319 in Japan after 1890. The stock of nonresidential structures rose much less, twenty-fold in the United Kingdom, thirty-two-fold in the United States, and eighty-three-fold in Japan.

Most machinery is power driven, but energy consumption rose much more slowly than the stock of machinery. In the United States, where there was an abundance of easily available timber in 1820, per capita consumption of primary energy has risen only threefold, against sixfold in the United Kingdom and twentyfold growth in Japan since 1820. Enormous progress has been made in the efficiency of energy conversion due to improvements in machines. Growth has also been underpinned by technical progress in locating and extracting energy from minerals. These now supply more than four-fifths of the world's energy supply. In 1820, the ratio was less than 6 percent, and 94 percent of world energy was derived from biomass (see related information in table 5).

In the course of the nineteenth century, great increases in the efficiency of steam engines were achieved by the development of compound and turbine technology. Landes (1965, 504–9) illustrated this by comparing the sixty-horsepower engine of a P&O paddle wheeler of 1829 with twin-turbines generating 136,000

TABLE 5
WORLD SUPPLY OF PRIMARY ENERGY, 1820–2001
(metric tons of oil equivalent)

	Modern Sources (million tons)	Biomass (million tons)	Total (million tons)	Population (million)	Per Capita (tons)
1820	12.9	208.2	221.1	1,041.1	0.21
1870	134.5	254.0	388.5	1,270.0	0.31
1913	735.2	358.2	1,093.4	1,791.0	0.61
1950	1,624.7	504.9	2,129.6	2,524.5	0.84
1973	5,368.8	673.8	6,042.6	3,913.5	1.54
2001	9,071.5	1,093.5	10,165.0	6,149.0	1.65

NOTE: Modern sources (coal, oil, natural gas, water, and atomic power); biomass (wood, peat, dung, straw, and other crop residues). Conversion coefficients, 1 ton of wood = 0.323 of oil; 1 ton of coal =0 .6458 ton of oil. 1973 and 1998 modern sources and biomass from International Energy Agency (2004a, 2004b). Modern sources 1870–1950 derived from Woytinsky and Woytinsky (1953), 1820 from Mitchell (1975). Biomass 1820–50 is assumed to be 0.20 ton per head of population, see Smil (1994, 185–87) for rough estimates of biomass back to 1700. My estimate of biomass 1820–1950 is somewhat lower than Smil suggests. In 1973, the world per-capita supply of biomass was 0.17 and in 1998 0.18 of a ton.

horsepower for the Cunard liner *Mauretania* in 1907. Thereafter, ships shifted increasingly to oil and diesel engines, which produced much more power than the same weight of coal and eliminated the need for stokers. Steam engines also revolutionized passenger and freight transport by land in the nineteenth century. Starting from scratch in 1826, almost a million kilometers of rail track had been built by 1913. The internal combustion engine reinforced the momentum of change, adding greatly to individual and family freedom of movement and choice in the location of industrial and commercial activity. In 1913, the fleet of passenger cars was about 1.5 million vehicles; by 1999, it was 520 million. In the second half of the twentieth century, air passenger miles rose from 28 billion in 1950 to 2.6 trillion in 1998. Development of electricity had at least as big an impact. It provided a multipurpose, efficient, and convenient source of heat, light, and power whose availability transformed household operation, office work, the nature and locus of industrial activity, and the potential for scientific research.

Human capital (i.e., the average number of years of education, weighted by level attained) rose by a factor of eleven in the United States and Japan and eight in the United Kingdom.

It was profitable to invest in this rapid expansion of physical and human capital because the rhythm of technical progress was much faster in the nineteenth and twentieth centuries than ever before. Some idea of the aggregate rate of technical progress can be derived by looking at the pace of advance in total factor productivity in the lead country. It was fastest in the period 1913–73 in the United States but has dropped off sharply since then, even though the technique of estimation of U.S. GDP has recently been modified to impute what seem to me excessive gains in the information technology sector.

International trade increased rapidly after 1820. The volume of exports per head of population rose 88-fold in the United Kingdom, 110-fold in the United States, and by a much higher proportion in Japan (whose economy was closed to foreign trade until 1855). It was important in enabling countries to specialize in the types of product in which they were most efficient. It eliminated the handicap of countries with limited natural resources. It was also important in diffusing new products and new technology.

The Roots of Modernity: Fundamental Features Underlying Western Ascension, 1000–1820

It is not possible to quantify the proximate causes of Western growth before 1820 in the detail shown in tables 4 and 5, but it is not difficult to identify the major changes in West European intellectual horizons and institutions, which were a fundamental prerequisite for the modest economic progress in this period and for the acceleration after 1820. From 1000 to 1820, investment in machinery and equipment was extremely modest. Investment in human capital was also modest, but the quality of human capital was transformed by the invention of printing, fundamental advances in science, and the spread of secular university education for the elites. Technical progress was slower than it is now, and much less capital intensive. Some of it derived from trial and error, but institutional support for scientific research had a very direct impact on technology, particularly in shipping and navigation. I have spelled out the changes in this domain in considerable detail, and explained how they were diffused among the major merchant capitalist empires. Technical progress in this period was not energy intensive. It relied on more effective wind power, improvements in the efficacy of horsepower, and an increase in hours worked per capita. There was very modest use of mineral fuels and heavy reliance on biomass. In proportionate terms, globalization was much more important from 1500 to 1870 than it has been since. A great part of the increase in productivity was due to gains from increased specialization and increases in the scale of production gains of the type stressed by Adam Smith in his analysis of the causes of economic progress up to 1776.

Four Major Intellectual and Institutional Changes in the West before 1820

There were four major intellectual and institutional changes in the West before 1820 that had a fundamental impact on economic performance and that had no counterpart in other parts of the world in this period.

a) A fundamental change was the recognition of human capacity to transform the forces of nature through rational investigation and experiment. The first European university was created in Bologna in 1080. By 1500, there were seventy such centers of secular learning in Western Europe (see Goodman and Russell 1991, 25). Until the mid-fifteenth century, most of the teaching was verbal, and the learning process was similar to that in ancient Greece. Things changed after Gutenberg printed his first book in Mainz in 1455. By 1500, 220 printing presses were in operation throughout Western Europe and had produced 8 million books (see Eisenstein 1993, 13–17). The productivity of universities and their openness to new ideas were greatly enlarged.

The main center of European publishing was Venice, where printed books were first produced in 1469. Before then, scribes, bookbinders, and specialists in ornamental calligraphy and illustration produced sacred books or translations of Greek and Latin classics for city archives or wealthy private collectors. Productivity in book production was revolutionized and costs had fallen dramatically by the 1470s. In 1483, the Ripoli press produced 1,025 copies of Plato's *Dialogues*. A scribe would have taken a year to produce one copy. Assuming that the Ripoli press had higher capital outlays on equipment than the institutions employing scribes and needed one man-year of skilled labor input to produce its 1,025 copies, one can infer that productivity in book production increased at least 200-fold. By the middle of the sixteenth century, the Venetian presses had produced some 20,000 titles, including music scores, maps, books on medical matters, and a flood of new secular learning. The latter point is of great significance. Before printing, books were cherished for their artistic or iconic value, and their content mainly reflected the wisdom and dogma of the past. Printing made books much cheaper. Publishers were much more willing to risk dissemination of new ideas and to provide an outlet for new authors. The proportion of the population with access to books was greatly increased, and there was a much greater incentive to aspire to literacy. It should also be stressed that, with the exception of China, the European printing revolution had no counterpart in most other parts of the world until the beginning of the nineteenth century. The major difference between Europe and China was the competitive character of European publishing and the international trade in books. This frustrated the attempts of the Papacy to achieve thought control through the Inquisition and censorship. China was a centralized state, with vestigial foreign contacts. The education of its bureaucracy was devoted to ancient classics, and they were able to exercise thought control by more subtle and effective methods than the Papacy in Europe.

Further changes in intellectual horizons occurred between the sixteenth and seventeenth centuries, when medieval notions of an earth-centered universe were abandoned. Thanks to the Renaissance, the seventeenth-century scientific revolution, and the eighteenth-century enlightenment, Western elites gradually abandoned superstition, magic, and submission to religious authority. The scientific approach gradually impregnated the educational system. Circumscribed intellectual horizons were abandoned. A Promethean quest for progress was unleashed. The impact of science was reinforced by the creation of scientific academies and observatories which inaugurated empirical research and experiment. Systematic recording of experimental results and their diffusion in written form were a key element in their success.

b) The emergence of important urban trading centers in Flanders and northern Italy in the eleventh and twelfth centuries was accompanied by changes that fostered entrepreneurship and abrogated feudal constraints on the purchase and sale of property. Nondiscretionary legal systems protected property rights. The development of accountancy helped further in making contracts enforceable. State fiscal levies became more predictable and less arbitrary. The growth of trustworthy financial institutions and instruments provided access to credit and insurance, which made it easier to assess risk and organize business rationally on a large scale over a wide area.

c) The adoption of Christianity as a state religion in 380 AD led to basic changes in the nature of European marriage, inheritance, and kinship. The Papacy imposed a pattern that differed substantially from what had prevailed earlier in Greece, Rome, and Egypt and differed dramatically from that which was to characterize the Islamic world. Marriage was to be strictly monogamous, with a ban on concubinage, adoption, divorce, and remarriage of widows. There was a prohibition on consanguineous marriage with siblings, ascendants, descendants, including first, second, and third cousins, or relatives of siblings by marriage. A Papal decision in 385 AD imposed priestly celibacy.

The main purpose of these rules was to limit inheritance entitlements to close family members and to channel large amounts to the church, which became a property owner on a huge scale. At the same time, they broke down previous loyalties to clan, tribe, or caste; promoted individualism and accumulation; and reinforced the sense of belonging to a nation-state (see Goody 1983; and Lal 2001).

d) A fourth distinctive feature was the emergence of a system of nation-states in close propinquity, that had significant trading relations and relatively easy intellectual interchange in spite of their linguistic differences. In many respects, this was a benign fragmentation. It stimulated competition and innovation. Migration to or refuge in a different culture and environment were options open to adventurous and innovative minds. However, the mercantilist commercial policies of the leading European countries were mutually discriminatory and restrictive. Beggar-your-neighbor policies were buttressed by wars. Between 1700 and 1820, the United Kingdom was involved five major wars (for a total of fifty-five years) due in large degree to its pursuit of worldwide commercial supremacy.

The Locus of Technical Change, 1000–1820

It is clear that sustained technical progress in navigation and ship-building was a major causal element in Western Europe's economic advance between 1000 and 1820. Without it, Western Europe would not have achieved its dominant role in world trade. It would not have strengthened its internal linkages via Mediterranean and Baltic trade; gone on to discover and take over huge areas of land, precious metals, and biological resources in the Americas; and captured a major share of Asian trade by circumnavigating Africa.

For the benefit of those who consider the period 1000 to 1820 to have been an era of technological stagnation, it is useful to scrutinize the evolution of shipping and navigational technology in some detail and to demonstrate the close interaction between science and technology from the sixteenth century onward.

Table 6 compares the growth of world trade and GDP from 1500 to 2001. The ratio between the two rates of growth is shown in the third column. The ratio was higher between 1500 and 1870 than it has been since.

Between 1470 and 1820, Western Europe's merchant fleet increased about seventeenfold. Per head of population, the rise was more than sixfold. Its effective carrying capacity rose more than this because of technical progress in design of ships, sails, and rigging; in improvements in instruments and techniques of navigation; in cartography; and in knowledge of geography, winds, and currents. Voyages became less dangerous for ships and their crews. Travel time became more predictable and regular, ships became bigger, and crew requirements per ton of cargo were reduced. European domination of the world's oceans was reinforced by advances in naval armament and the capacity to organize business on a large scale in ventures that required significant capital outlays over a relatively long period.

In the year 1000, Mediterranean ships were no better than and navigation inferior to the situation a thousand years earlier. Ships were rigged with square sails, which were efficient only when the

TABLE 6

GLOBALIZATION RATIO: COMPARATIVE GROWTH IN THE
VOLUME OF WORLD TRADE AND GDP, 1500–2001
(annual average compound growth rates)

	World Trade	World GDP	Col. 1/Col. 2
1500–1820	0.96	0.32	3.0
1820–70	4.18	0.93	4.5
1870–1913	3.40	2.11	1.6
1913–50	0.90	1.82	0.5
1950–73	7.88	4.90	1.6
1973–2001	5.22	3.05	1.7
1820–2001	3.93	2.22	1.8

SOURCE: World trade volume 1500–1820 is derived from growth in tonnage of the world merchant fleet (Maddison 2001, 95), with a 50 percent upward adjustment for technical improvements that augmented effective carrying capacity; 1820–70 from Maddison (1982, 254); 1870–2001 from Maddison (2001, 362), updated to 2001 from *International Monetary Fund*, International Financial Statistics. World GDP from Maddison (2003a). See O'Rourke and Williamson (2002) for a similar estimate of the growth in intercontinental trade volume for 1500–1800, obtained by a totally different approach.

wind was astern. Voyages against the wind could be extremely lengthy and uncertain. Harbor facilities were inferior to those constructed by the Emperor Claudius at Portus for the food supply of Rome, and Alexandria's great port and lighthouse had disappeared. Some navigational aids were the same as in Roman times—lead lines for sounding the depth of water and a wind rose that helped identify the direction of winds. The stars and the sun provided guidance on position and time of day. There were no charts or sailing instructions showing depths, anchorages, and tides of the kind the Greeks and Romans had.

In the thirteenth century, there were significant improvements. The most important was the magnetic compass showing thirty-two directional points, somewhat like a wind rose, but with a pointer directed continuously to the north. A sternpost rudder replaced trailing oars as a more effective means of steering. The power of rudders was strengthened by use of cranks and pulleys, making it much easier to maintain course in bad weather. There were improvements in Mediterranean sails, notably the use of the Arab lateen rig set at an angle to the mast, instead of a rectangular sail set square to the mast. This made it possible to sail in a wider range of wind conditions and reduced the time spent idling in port or at anchor. The Venetian sandglass made it possible to measure the elapse of time accurately over a given interval. Wooden traverse boards allowed mariners to plot the course of a voyage. The board had a face like a compass, with eight holes at each compass point and eight pegs attached to the center. At each half hour of the four-hour watch, a peg was placed in the appropriate hole to indicate the course of the ship in that interval. Traverse tables provided trig-onometrical guidance in estimating daily progress, and calculation was made easier by the adoption of Arabic numerals. About the same time, *portolans* (charts with an indication of ports, tides, depths, and winds) began to appear. They provided sailing instruc-tions derived from the experience of earlier mariners. They showed coastal outlines and distances between ports, with an array of alter-native courses (rhumb lines). Even if none of the lines was appro-priate for the intended voyage, each nevertheless helped the mariner design and pursue his own trajectory, using a ruler and dividers. *Portolans* were made of vellum (a single sheepskin up to five feet long and half as wide) with directions inscribed in black and red ink.

These changes increased the productivity of Venetian ships, which had previously not ventured the trip to Egypt between Octo-ber and April, when the sky was frequently overcast. With these instruments, a ship could make two return journeys a year from Venice to Alexandria instead of one.

Similarly, innovations in shipbuilding reduced costs and improved efficiency. In Roman times, the hull had been constructed first. Ships were held together by a careful watertight cabinetwork of mortise and tenon. The second stage was the insertion of ribs and braces. From the eleventh century, the keel and ribs were built first, and a hull of nailed planks was added, using fiber and pitch to make the hull watertight.

In the fifteenth century, the locus of maritime progress switched to Portugal, which was exploring the Atlantic islands and the

African coast. Major changes in rigging permitted sails to harness wind energy with much greater efficiency than in earlier Mediterranean vessels. With more masts and a much more complex array of sails, ships became more maneuverable and faster. They could tack into the wind with much greater ease. The Venetian galley, whose motive power depended on oarsmen, became obsolete. A new type of vessel, the caravel, was more robust and able to operate successfully in the stormier seas and stronger currents of the Atlantic.

The Portuguese made major progress in navigation, developing new instruments and much better charts. In the Northern Hemisphere, the pole star provided a more or less constant bearing and altitude. On a north-south passage, a navigator could observe the pole star each day at dawn and dusk (when he could see both the star and the horizon). By noting changes in altitude, he could get some idea of changes in his position. In sailing east-west, he could keep a steady course by maintaining a constant polar altitude. All this had been done very crudely, using finger spreads or other rough means of measuring altitude. In the fifteenth century, the Portuguese developed the quadrant, which made it possible to judge latitudes and distance sailed. They also devised techniques of correction for the slight rotation of the polar star. In the Southern Hemisphere, which Portuguese ships had begun to enter, there was no star with the same properties, and the sun was used instead of the polar star. The sun's altitude could not be measured with a quadrant, as its light was too bright for the naked eye, so a variant of the astronomer's astrolabe was developed for mariners. Because of the earth's movement, the altitude of the sun was different every day, so altitude readings had to be adjusted for daily changes in the sun's declination. These tables were constructed by the astronomer Zacuto in the 1470s. After practical tests of the instruments and tables on trial voyages, a naval almanac, *Regimento do Astrolabio et do Quadrante*, was compiled and used by Vasco da Gama when he sailed to India in 1497. In the fifteenth century, there were improvements in measuring speed and distance traveled at sea. The nautical mile became the standard unit of distance, and the log-line that trailed from the stern was marked by knots spaced uniformly to mark fractions of a mile. The running time of the sandglass was adjusted to match.

European knowledge of world geography was revolutionized by the establishment of the new routes in the Southern Hemisphere, the discovery of the Americas, and Ferdinand Magellan's circumnavigation of the globe. New maps were needed, charts were improved, atlases began to appear, and the invention of printing greatly facilitated their diffusion. Globes were produced to give a more accurate idea of world geography on long routes. In 1569, the Flemish mapmaker Gerard Mercator developed a projection technique to represent the world's sphericity on a flat surface. On his charts, parallels of latitude and meridians of longitude cut each other at right angles. Meridians were spread apart as they approached the poles. As a counterbalance, the spacing of latitude degrees was increased progressively toward the poles. As a result, the line of a constant compass bearing was straight. This was of great potential use for navigators, but was not widely adopted until the seventeenth century. Calculation of a ship's course was greatly simplified by Napier's 1614 invention of logarithms, which became available to mariners in the form of decimal tables, invented by Briggs in 1631. Logarithmic slide rules were available to mariners from the middle of the seventeenth century, along with other trigonometric shortcuts. In 1594, the English navigator John Davis invented a simple backstaff that could be used to measure solar altitude without sighting the sun directly. By the end of the seventeenth century, it had replaced the seaman's quadrant and astrolabe. It was superseded by a much more precise reflecting octant invented by the English mathematician Halley in 1731 as a by-product of his work on reflecting telescopes. This was further improved by the British Navy's sextant in 1757, which permitted a quick and accurate reading of any celestial object against the horizon.

The search for accurate measurement of longitude had been under way for a long time. Philip III of Spain offered large financial rewards in 1598, and similar incentives had been offered in France and Holland. In 1714, the British government created a Board of Longitude, which offered a £20,000 prize for an invention accurate within narrow specifications. The prize was won by John Harrison, who, after twenty-five years of effort, made a chronometer in 1760 (about twice the size of a pocket watch) that was unaffected by the movement of a ship and changes in the weather. This was success-fully tested in trials to the West Indies in 1762–64. Captain Cook, who had used the new *Nautical Almanac* and the lunar method of estimating longitude in his first Pacific voyage in 1768–71, used a copy of Harrison's watch on his 1772–75 trip around the world. When he returned to Plymouth after three years of sailing, his cumulative error in longitude was less than eight miles.

By the end of the eighteenth century, great progress had been made in the design of ships and rigging, in gunnery, in meteoro-logical and astronomical knowledge, and in the precision of navi-gational instruments. Maps had been enormously improved and were supplemented by detailed coastal surveys. Sailing had become safer, the duration of voyages was more predictable, and the inci-dence of shipwreck had fallen significantly. There was also progress in reducing disease mortality on long voyages.

In his voyage around the world in 1740–44, Anson successfully harried the Spanish in the Pacific and captured a huge treasure ship with loss of only 4 men by enemy action, but 1,300 fell victim to disease, mainly scurvy. This led the British naval physician James Lind to carry out dietary experiments. In 1753 he published his results and recommended orange and lemon juice as a preventive measure. Captain Cook, in his voyage of 1768–71, experimented with a number of antiscorbutic items, including oranges, lemons, and sauerkraut. He had only one case of scurvy, but it was not until 1795 that regular issue of lemon juice was adopted by the Royal Navy.

European naval weaponry and modes of warfare had changed completely by the sixteenth century. The oared galley, which was used for close combat, ramming, and boarding, was last used at the battle of Lepanto in 1571. It was replaced by ships maneuver-able enough to engage the enemy at a distance with broadsides from heavy artillery pieces. Bronze guns were replaced by much-improved and cheaper iron weaponry.

At first, naval guns were fired from the superstructure, and the size of ships was enlarged to maximize firepower. Very large ships of this kind (the English *Harry Grace à Dieu*, 1514; the French *Grand François*, 1534; the Portuguese *São Jão*, 1552; and the Swedish *Elefanten*, 1559) were unstable and sank very quickly. The British developed a more successful design around 1550, the galleon. This medium-sized, fast, and maneuverable ship had guns on the lower decks that fired through ports in the hull. It proved successful in 1588 against bigger ships in the Spanish Armada. The Dutch also found it effective against the large carracks that the Portuguese used in their Asian trade.

The Scientific Revolution

From the middle of the sixteenth century to the end of the seventeenth, there was fundamental progress in Western science that had important consequences for navigation and brought revolutionary changes in European perceptions of the universe, the interaction of the earth, the other planets, the sun, and the stars. The revolution started in 1543 with the publication of Copernicus's heliocentric theory rejecting the scholastic notion that the earth was the center of the universe. This was followed by detailed observation of the movement of celestial bodies and recognition of the nature and mutability of their orbits by Kepler and Galileo, estimates of celestial distance, and new conclusions about the laws of motion. Beginning in 1610, Galileo made his own refractor telescopes and used them to observe the mountains and craters of the moon, the spots on the sun, the satellites of Jupiter, the phases of Venus, and the stars of the Milky Way. His quarter-century of observation greatly enriched the empirical evidence for the Copernican hypothesis. In 1632, he published his *Dialogue on the Two Chief Systems of the World* (Ptolemaic and Copernican). As a result, he was detained by the Church authorities, who regarded him as a heretic, and, under threat of torture, Galileo was forced to recant. He remained sequestered, and his works were banned by Papal decree until 1757. The counterreformation Papacy was militant in its persecution of heresy and heretical books. The Jesuit order and the Inquisition were major instruments of this policy, and intellectual freedom in Italy was further weakened by Spanish control of Lombardy and the kingdom of Naples.

In the mid-seventeenth century, the locus of the scientific revolution moved to northern Europe, notably England, France, and Holland. The climax was Newton's *Principia*, published in 1687, which showed that the whole universe was subject to the same laws of motion and gravitation. Newton's conclusions, like Galileo's, were carefully tested against empirical evidence of celestial phenomena. He constructed a new type of reflecting telescope for his own observations and followed closely the results of research in the Royal Society, founded in London in 1662 (he was president of the society from 1703 to 1727). The French Académie des Sciences was created shortly after. Astronomical research in both institutions was buttressed by astronomical observatories. The Paris Observatory was established in 1672 and the Greenwich Observatory in 1695. Interaction between the two academies was close. Newton was influenced by the research at the French Academy by the Dutch scientist Huygens and the precise measurements of celestial distance by Picard and Cassini at the Paris Observatory.

Progress in astronomy and physics was accompanied by major advances in mathematics and design of new instruments (telescopes, micrometers, microscopes, thermometers, barometers, air pumps, clocks and watches, and the steam engine) that had important implications for the progress of navigation. Their practical implications for seamanship were the particular domain of the British Navy and Greenwich Observatory. They were also part of Colbert's efforts to reconstruct the French navy from 1669 onward.

The link between scientific research and practical matters of navigation is clear from the work of Edmond Halley (1656–1742). He wrote his first paper for the Royal Society in 1676, when he was nineteen. It dealt with irregularities he had observed in the orbits of the planets Jupiter and Saturn, which were believed to be uniformly elliptic. Over the next sixty-five years, he wrote another eighty scientific papers while serving as secretary of the Royal Society, professor of geometry at Oxford, and astronomer royal (see MacPike, 1932). Among other contributions, he encouraged Newton to finish his *Principia*, financed its publication, and checked the proofs. He was an honorary member of the French Académie des Sciences from 1729 onward.

In 1677, Halley went to St. Helena for eighteen months to make the first catalogue of stars observable in the Southern Hemisphere. He used a telescope with a micrometer to measure their position and coordinates. In 1679, the Royal Society sent him to Danzig to check the accuracy of Hevelius's catalogue of stars visible in the Northern Hemisphere. From 1680 to 1705, he made a comparative analysis of the orbits of twenty-four comets, explained the reasons for their apparently erratic variation, and predicted correctly the return of Halley's comet in 1758. He studied the orbits of the planets Mercury and Venus, which are nearer to the sun than the earth is. He used his 1677 observation of the transit of Mercury to make a crude measure of the sun's distance from the earth. In 1691, he predicted transits of Venus for 1761 and 1769 and suggested that they be observed at extreme points of the earth in order to measure the dimensions of the solar system. His suggestions were implemented, and Cook observed the 1769 transit during his expedition to Tahiti.

Halley made three important contributions of great practical significance for mariners. Between 1683 and 1715, he measured the earth's atmosphere, the causes of variation in air pressure, and the origins of trade winds and monsoons. He produced the first meteorological chart of wind patterns in the Atlantic, Indian, and Pacific oceans in 1686. He followed this by studies of rates of evaporation and replenishment of water. He estimated the daily evaporation of water in the Mediterranean to be 5.3 billion tons and analyzed the ways this was replaced by rainfall and river flows.

In 1683, he started collecting observations of variance in terrestrial magnetism (which caused puzzling effects on compass readings) He speculated on their origin at different levels below the earth's surface and the effect of the earth's rotation. In 1698–1700, he directed a naval expedition in the Atlantic to measure magnetic variation systematically, and in 1701 published the first chart showing isogonic lines of equal magnetic variation distributed over the earth's surface. Thereafter, charts of this kind became an essential part of the navigator's equipment.

Halley's third major contribution was painstaking daily lunar observation over a period of two decades to provide tables for accurate measurement of longitude. The results were incorporated in the annual *Nautical Almanac*, published at Greenwich from 1767 onward.

The scientific revolution had a very direct influence on European navigation and capacity to penetrate distant oceans. It was of fundamental long-term importance in virtually all areas of activity. Advances in knowledge were closely linked with empirical investigation and the production of precision instruments (such as telescopes, microscopes, clocks, and watches). The revolution in cosmology stirred the European imagination and promoted Promethean ambitions.

These developments in Europe were an essential prelude to the much faster economic development that occurred in the nineteenth and twentieth centuries. They had no counterpart in other parts of the world.

PART II

The European Transformation of the Americas, 1500–1820

The European Encounter and Its Impact

When contact was first established, the Americas were thinly settled. The population was a third of the European and the land area eleven times as large. The technological level was greatly inferior. There were no wheeled vehicles, draught animals, sailing ships, metal tools, weapons, or ploughs. There were no cattle, sheep, pigs, or hens. The most densely populated areas (Mexico and Peru) had significant urban centers and a sophisticated vegetarian agriculture. Elsewhere, most of the inhabitants were hunter-gatherers.

American populations had no resistance to diseases Europeans brought (smallpox, measles, influenza, and typhus) or African diseases (yellow fever and malaria), which arrived shortly afterward. By the middle of the sixteenth century, two-thirds were wiped out. The mortality rate was twice that of Europe during the Black Death of the fourteenth century.[4]

The two advanced civilizations (Aztec in Mexico and Inca in Peru) were destroyed. Their populations were reduced to anomie and serfdom. Hunter-gatherer populations elsewhere were marginalized or exterminated. The conquest of the Americas was unequivocal. The economy of these relatively empty lands was completely revamped. The hemisphere was repopulated by the arrival of nearly 8 million African slaves between 1500 and 1820 and about 2 million European settlers. In 1820, 41 percent of the population was white, 26 percent

31

TABLE 7

ECONOMIES OF THE AMERICAS, FIVE REGIONS, 1500–2001
(population in thousands; per capita GDP in 1990 international dollars;
GDP in millions of 1990 international dollars)

	1500	1600	1700	1820	2001
Mexico					
Population	7,500	2,500	4,500	6,587	101,879
Per capita GDP	425	454	568	759	7,089
GDP	3,188	1,134	2,558	5,000	722,198
15 other Spanish American countries (excluding Caribbean)					
Population	8,500	5,100	5,800	7,691	212,919
Per capita GDP	412	432	498	683	5,663
GDP	3,500	2,201	2,889	5,255	1,205,630
30 Caribbean countries					
Population	500	200	500	2,920	38,650
Per capita GDP	400	430	650	636	4,373
GDP	200	86	325	1,857	169,032
Brazil					
Population	1,000	800	1,250	4,507	177,753
Per capita GDP	400	428	459	646	5,570
GDP	400	342	574	2,912	990,076
Total Latin America					
Population	17,500	8,600	12,050	21,705	531,201
Per capita GDP	416	438	527	692	5,811
GDP	7,288	3,763	6,346	15,024	3,086,936
United States and Canada					
Population	2,250	1,750	1,200	10,797	316,617
Per capita GDP	400	400	511	1,231	27,384
GDP	900	700	613	13,286	8,670,389

Source: Maddison (2003a, 114).

indigenous, 22 percent black or mulatto, and 11 percent *mestizo* (see tables 7 and 8). The high proportion of whites in 1820 indicates who benefited from the transformation of the Americas. European settlers

TABLE 8
ETHNIC COMPOSITION OF THE AMERICAS AND THE CARIBBEAN, 1820
(thousands of inhabitants)

	Indigenous	Mestizo	Black and Mulatto	White	Total
Americas					
Mexico	3,570	1,777	10	1,230	6,587
Brazil	500		2,500	1,507	4,507
Caribbean			2,366	554	2,920
Other Latin America	4,000	1,800	400	1,485	7,685
United States	325		1,772	7,884	9,981
Canada	75			741	816
Total	8,470	3,577	7,048	13,401	32,496
Caribbean					
Cuba and Puerto Rico (Spanish)			453	400	853
Haiti and Dominican Republic (independent)			742	70	812
British colonies			827	53	880
French colonies			230	20	250
Dutch colonies			74	6	80
Danish and Swedish colonies			40	5	45
Total			2,366	554	2,920

SOURCE: Mexico from Maddison (1995b, 315–316); Brazil from Maddison (2001, 235); United States from Maddison (2001, 250); Canada from Maddison (2001, 180); other Latin America from Maddison (2001, 235), excluding Caribbean; Cuba and Puerto Rico from Shepherd and Beckles (2000, 274, 285); Haiti and Dominican Republic (independent in 1804 and 1821, respectively), French, Dutch, Danish, and Swedish colonies derived from Engerman and Higman (1997); British colonies from Higman (1984). Caribbean includes British Guiana and Suriname.

had higher fertility, longer life expectation, and much higher average incomes than African slaves and the indigenous population.

Although the initial impact of conquest and colonization was massively destructive, the long-term economic potential was greatly enhanced. Capacity to support a bigger population was augmented by the introduction of new crops and animals (see Crosby, 1972). The new items were wheat, rice, sugar cane, vines, cabbages, lettuce, olives, bananas, yams, and coffee. The new animals for food were cattle, pigs, chickens, sheep, and goats. The introduction of transport and traction animals—horses, oxen, asses, and mules—along with wheeled vehicles and plows (which replaced digging sticks) were a major contribution to productive capacity. There was a reciprocal transfer of New World crops to Europe, Asia, and Africa—maize, potatoes, sweet potatoes, manioc, chilies, tomatoes, peanuts, lima and string beans, pineapples, cocoa, and tobacco—which enhanced the rest of the world's production and capacity to sustain population growth.

Population and output recovered somewhat in the seventeenth century but in 1700 were still well below 1500 levels. Growth accelerated rapidly in the eighteenth century; aggregate population, per capita income, and total GDP rose much faster than anywhere else in the world. The 1820 level of GDP was more than three times that of 1500, and average per-capita income was well above the world average. The economy, technology, and economic institutions of the Americas had been transformed. Large parts were relatively empty, still pushing out the frontier of settlement, but most of the continent had achieved political independence in nation-states still recognizable today.

The Americas continued to grow faster than the rest of the world economy. In 1820, they accounted for less than 4 percent of world GDP; by 2001, they were nearly a third. Between 1820 and 2001, there was net immigration of 80 million people.

There was significant variance in the per capita growth trajectory of different parts of the Americas. A good deal was due to differences in the nature of the colonial regimes and the institutions and social structures they created:

a) Spain concentrated its main activity on Mexico and Peru, which were the most densely populated at the time of conquest. Docile indigenous populations were compelled to supply labor to mining and agriculture. Slave imports were comparatively modest (about 1.5 million over the whole period of Spanish rule). The main aims were to transfer a fiscal tribute (in precious metals) to Spain and to hispanicize and catholicize the indigenous population.

b) Portuguese objectives were much more commercial, developing plantation agriculture for export. As the indigenous people of Brazil were hunter-gatherers and hard to capture, the colonial labor force was composed largely of African slaves. Between 1500 and 1870, 3.8 million were transported to Brazil.

c) The Dutch, British, and French introduced plantation agriculture in Caribbean islands they seized from Spain in the seventeenth century. The indigenous populations had been virtually exterminated before they arrived, 3.8 million slaves were imported in the colonial period, and production became highly specialized. A large part of the food supply was imported, and per capita exports were much higher than elsewhere in the Americas. The number of white settlers was relatively small, and they were occupied mainly in supervising slave labor. Plantation owners were a wealthy absentee elite, living mainly in their respective metropoles.

d) North America had a substantial neo-European economy, where abundant land and natural resources were exploited by European labor. Virginia, Maryland, and the Carolinas relied on slave labor for their tobacco and cotton plantations, but the slave proportion was smaller, the climate healthier, and the workload lighter than in Caribbean sugar production. As a consequence, the life expectancy of slaves was longer and slave imports much smaller (about 400,000). The sociopolitical order of the northern colonies permitted much freer access to land and education than in Spanish America, Brazil, and the Caribbean, with a smaller drain of tribute and profit to the metropole.

European Gains from the Americas

There were seven main types of economic gain to Europe:

1. A new supply of precious metals (about 1,700 tons of gold and 73,000 tons of silver). About a third of this was destined to finance European imports from Asia.

2. Imports of exotic products—sugar, tobacco, cotton, coffee, and cocoa from the slave colonies.

3. Imports from the northern colonies of fish, furs, ships, timber, and other materials required for shipbuilding.

4. Export markets for European manufactures.

5. Profits from the slave trade.

6. Opportunities for European migration to a continent with much greater per capita land availability.

7. Windfall ecological benefits flowing from the transfer of indigenous American plants. For Europe, the most important were maize and potatoes. Maize and manioc went to raise Africa's capacity to sustain population growth. Sweet potatoes, peanuts, and maize served the same purpose in China.

Spanish Policy and Institutions

Spain followed a policy of conquest imperialism, exterminated the Aztec and Inca elites and their priesthood, and seized their property. Large estates (*encomiendas*) were allocated to a privileged elite of Spaniards, giving them control of the labor of a traumatized Indian population.[5] Churches and convents were built on the ruins of Aztec and Inca temples. The main agents of social control were the religious orders. The old gods, calendars, records, relics, and institutions disappeared in the process of catholicization.

A major reason for this approach was long experience in the reconquest of territory from the Moors. Spain had the military know-how and organization for conquest and a church experienced in evangelizing, converting, and indoctrinating a conquered population. Islam and Judaism were proscribed in Spain, just as the Inca and Aztec religions were extirpated in Mexico. Furthermore, the church in Spain was firmly under national control; the king was free to appoint bishops under a sixteenth-century treaty with the Papacy. Centuries of militant struggle had concentrated power and legitimacy on the Spanish monarchy as the ultimate arbiter, against which rebellion, even in very distant colonies, was seldom imagined.

In the sixteenth century, the bulk of European trade with the Americas was Spanish. Initially, it was concentrated on the Caribbean islands, where gold was available from alluvial deposits and there were experiments with plantation agriculture. The main locus of activity shifted after the discovery of rich silver deposits at Potosí in the Viceroyalty of Peru in 1545, and at Zacatecas (1546) and Guanajuato (1548) in the Viceroyalty of New Spain.[6] The economic value of these mines was greatly enhanced by application of the new mercury amalgamation process. This cold procedure permitted high rates of extraction from low-grade ores at much lower cost than earlier fuel-intensive techniques.

Development of the mines required huge investment, transport over large distances, and massive inputs of Indian labor. The industry was developed and financed by Genoese and German bankers who made substantial remittances to Europe. A 20 percent tax (*quinto real*) was levied on the value of silver. Proceeds of the quinto and other levies permitted large state transfers to Spain. From the second half of the seventeenth century, there were also large illicit shipments to destinations other than Spain (see Morineau, 1985).

The logistics of silver production were most complex in the Viceroyalty of Peru. The Potosí mine (in present-day Bolivia) was 13,000 feet above sea level. Mercury was discovered and developed at Huancavelica, but had to be moved 1,600 kilometers to the mines in skin bags (a two-month journey on the back of llamas or mules). Silver was moved by pack animal from the mines to Callao (the port of Lima) or Arica to be shipped up the Pacific coast. It was then transported by pack animal to the port of Nombre de Dios (later Portobello) on the Caribbean side of the isthmus of Panama for shipment to Seville. In Mexico, mercury was shipped to the mines from Almadén in Spain and the silver transported to Veracruz on the Atlantic coast.

Shipments to Spain were made in annual convoys, with armed escort vessels. In addition to silver, exports included hides and leather, dyestuffs, sugar, and tobacco. All traffic was funneled into and out of Spain via Seville (replaced by Cádiz in the eighteenth century), and virtually all traffic from or to the Americas went via Veracruz in Mexico, Portobello in Panama, and Cartagena in present-day Colombia. Trade on these routes was reserved to Spanish ships. The organization of convoys was closely supervised and controlled by the *Casa de Contratación* in Seville. Exports via Seville consisted of Spanish wine, olive oil, furniture, cloth, paper, and iron wares, but reexports of French textiles and manufactures of other European countries were usually much bigger. There were restrictions on manufactures in the colonies; production of wine and oil was permitted in Peru but not in New Spain. Spain itself shipped very few slaves until late in the eighteenth century. When slaves were wanted, the trade was subcontracted initially to Portugal (Treaty of Tordesillas, 1494), and later to the British (Treaty of Utrecht, 1713). Trade with Asia was limited to the annual galleon that left Acapulco for Manila, loaded with silver. The return cargo consisted mainly of Chinese silks. Trade between Manila and China was done mainly by Chinese merchants.

The inflow of silver had a limited impact in strengthening the Spanish economy. Some financed the construction of baroque churches and palaces. Much more went to finance Spain's hegemonic commitments in Europe. The government waged an eighty-year war trying to reconquer the Netherlands. It launched a huge armada in 1588 in an unsuccessful attempt to invade England. It had to defend its territorial possessions in Italy (Naples, Sicily, and the Duchy of Milan), parts of northern France, Franche Comté, and the southern Netherlands (Belgium). From 1580 to 1640, it ruled

Portugal. It was a major protagonist in wars to restrain the expansion of the Ottoman Empire. The government was the most zealous agent of the counterreformation, using the Inquisition to ban books, burn heretics, and expel converted Jews and Muslims (new Christians and Moriscos) from Spain. These policies weakened intellectual development, commercial life, and agriculture.

Twice in the sixteenth century the government defaulted on debt. On several occasions it confiscated private shipments of bullion, compensating the owners with worthless government bonds. This induced large-scale smuggling by merchants and traders in the colonies, who understated their shipments of silver to Spain or shipped it elsewhere in Europe to avoid taxes and seizures by British, Dutch, and French corsairs.

In the sixteenth century, the number of ships leaving Spain for the Americas averaged fifty-eight a year (see Usher 1932, 206). By the mid-seventeenth century, the fleet system "was a shell of its former self, sailing late in the season, unable to sail for years at a time, composed of ageing and unsafe ships, many of them built abroad" (Macleod 1984, 372). In the seventeenth century, Spain's economy stagnated. Population growth was checked by attacks of plague and hunger. It suffered defeats in land and sea battles trying to retain its European empire. Administrative control in Spain and the colonies was costly and inefficient. The reign of Charles II (1664–1700), a near imbecile, was "an unmitigated disaster, a bleak chronicle of military defeat, royal bankruptcy, intellectual regression and widespread famine" (Brading 1984, 389).

On the death of this last Spanish Habsburg, France installed a Bourbon monarch, Philip V. After the long War of Spanish Succession (1701–13), he was eventually recognized by other European powers, but the peace treaty forced Spain to cede Milan, Sardinia, Naples, and the Spanish Netherlands (Belgium) to Austria; Sicily to the kingdom of Savoy; and Gibraltar and Minorca to Britain, which acquired commodity and slave trading rights in the Americas.

The seventeenth-century decline of Spanish power and income did little damage to the colonies. Silver output continued, and the colonial elite retained a larger part of the profit. As Spanish control weakened, local industries developed; trade between the colonies and contraband trade with other European countries and their colonies became significant.

Expanded use of European crops and livestock and the abundance of land facilitated the growth of agriculture and the area of settlement. Wheeled transport, commercial activity, and urbanization increased. Creoles (whites born in the Americas) and mestizos (offspring or descendants of unions between whites and the indigenous population) were a rapidly increasing proportion of the population and became local oligarchies, buying administrative and judicial offices. Spanish district officials (*corregidores*) depended on bribes for most of their income. Regulations were bent and tax burdens softened to accommodate the interests of the creole population. They had lower incomes than the much smaller elite group of *peninsulares* (Spanish civil servants, judiciary, military, and clergy), but they were more prosperous than most of the population in Spain. The indigenous population was an underclass, with the legal status of minors. Most were rural. Some provided cheap labor for haciendas or mines; most lived in isolated villages, engaged in subsistence agriculture.

In the eighteenth century, the Bourbon regime increased the efficiency of administration and resource allocation in Spain. The population increased considerably, and there was some growth in per capita income. It also revamped its administration and improved resource allocation in the Americas. Trade and government revenue from the Americas increased. In 1748–78, ship sailings to the Americas averaged seventy-four a year, compared with thirty-three between 1718 and 1747. In 1739, a new Viceroyalty of New Granada (the area which is now Venezuela, Colombia, and Ecuador) was carved out of the old Viceroyalty of Peru. In 1776, Peru was further truncated to create a new Viceroyalty of La Plata with its capital at Buenos Aires (including present-day Argentina, Bolivia, Chile, Paraguay, and Uruguay), and Venezuela was given greater autonomy within New Granada. These changes led to a significant reorientation of trade to the benefit of the expanding economies of Buenos Aires and Venezuela and to the detriment of

Lima. Taxation of mining was changed to increase production incentives, and Mexican silver production rose substantially. Sales taxes were collected directly, rather than by tax farmers, and their incidence was raised. Government control of tobacco taxes was strengthened. There were important moves to free trade. The clumsy and expensive fleet system was abolished in 1778. Trade was permitted between all Spanish and colonial ports. In 1789, restrictions on the slave trade were ended.

Between 1763 and 1795, there were major changes in the mode of colonial governance to tighten Spain's control and increase its revenues. *Intendentes*, a new type of paid official, replaced the *corregidores*. These posts were filled by peninsular Spaniards. There was closer control of town councils (*cabildos*) and a major shake-up of the higher judiciary. Most of the judgeships in the *audiencias* had been sold to wealthy Creole lawyers, who were replaced by a career service of peninsular Spaniards. The role of local militias was reduced in favor of the regular army. In 1767, all Jesuit priests were expelled from Spain and the Americas. The government seized and sold the colossal assets of their order and took over the administration of Paraguay, which the Jesuits had controlled for two centuries. As they had provided cheap mortgages and other financial services, this was not a popular move in the colonies. Subsequently, the privileges and immunities of the other clergy were substantially reduced.

The Bourbon reforms alienated the local Creole elite, and independence became more readily conceivable than in earlier centuries. The British colonies of North America had achieved independence, and the *ancien régime* had collapsed in France. However, Creoles were reluctant to revolt because the very unequal social structure increased the risk of takeover by mestizos or the indigenous population. This apprehension was greatest in Peru, where there had been an indigenous revolt (Tupac Amaru) in 1780, and in Mexico, where there was an Indian insurrection in 1810.

The move to independence was reinforced by events in Spain. In 1793, after the execution of Louis XVI, Spain joined an international coalition against France. After its defeat in 1795, Spain switched sides, became a subservient ally of France, and declared war on England. Britain mounted a very successful blockade of trade with the Americas, sank the Spanish fleet at Trafalgar, and briefly occupied Buenos Aires. In 1808, Ferdinand VII forced his father, Charles IV, to abdicate in his favor. Almost immediately, he himself was forced to abdicate in favor of Napoleon's brother Joseph, who was sustained in power until 1813 by French occupation troops. Ferdinand was kept captive in France. The French takeover was contested by popular uprisings and creation of municipal juntas as centers of resistance. By 1810, the effectively functioning resistance forces were confined to the city of Cádiz, where a council of regency convoked a parliament (Cortés) to draft a liberal constitution in 1812. This held out the promise of a constitutional monarchy in Spain, but proposed to retain a subservient status for the colonies.

The French regime was not regarded as legitimate in Latin America, and control by the metropole had effectively collapsed. Creole elites in Caracas, Bogotá, Buenos Aires, and Santiago stepped into the vacuum. They converted their municipal councils into juntas and took over their administration, without renouncing their theoretical allegiance to Spain. They faced opposition from the old officialdom and military to a degree that varied in different parts of the continent. The imperial authorities in Peru and Venezuela were their most ferocious opponents..

In 1814, Ferdinand VII returned from exile in France, repudiated the liberal constitution, and acted as an absolute monarch. He dispatched 10,000 troops to repress the opposition forces in Venezuela. He would have been better advised to try conciliation. His efforts provoked intensified resistance and the emergence of effective republican armies led by San Martin in the south and Bolivar in the north. Ferdinand tried to send reinforcements from Spain in 1820, but his troops rebelled instead of embarking. By 1826, the last Spanish forces surrendered, freeing more than 14 million people from Spanish rule. In 1790, the Spanish empire had covered 16.1 million square kilometers; now, Cuba and Puerto Rico were all that was left (123,000 square kilometers and less than 700,000 people). Nine new nations emerged in the south with a population of 6.6 million. Newly independent Mexico had 6.5 million, and the five small countries of Central America formed a temporary union. Louisiana had been ceded to Napoleon in 1800, and he sold it to the United States in 1803. Florida had been ceded to the United States in 1819.

With independence, the old bureaucracy and military disappeared, along with the Inquisition and the remittance of fiscal tribute to Spain. The Creoles took over political power, but the struggle for independence had damaged the economies, exacerbated social tension, and led to decades of economic instability. Bolivar had hoped to create a Latin American federation and was deeply disappointed by the mutual hostility between the new states. Unstable governments relied on military force as a sanction for power. More than half the population remained an indigenous underclass with no legal rights or access to education and property. The independence of Latin America was recognized by the United Kingdom and the United States in 1823. The Papacy delayed until 1835. Spain began to acknowledge it in 1836 but took several decades to finalize the process.

As a result of political chaos, Mexico had seventy-one rulers (elected and unelected) between 1821 and 1876 and more than 200 ministers of finance. In the same period, the United States had fourteen presidents and twenty-six secretaries of the Treasury and took over half of Mexico's territory. Mexican per capita income was lower in 1877 than in 1820 (see figure 2a on page 53 for a comparison of the development of per-capita income in Mexico and the United States, 1700–2001).

Portuguese Policy and Institutions

When the Portuguese arrived in Brazil in 1500, they did not find an advanced civilization with hoards of precious metals for plunder or a social discipline and organization geared to provide steady tribute that they could appropriate. Brazilian Indians were mainly hunter-gatherers, though some were moving toward agriculture using slash-and-burn techniques to cultivate manioc. Their technology and resources meant that they were thin on the ground. They had no towns and no domestic animals. They were stone-age men and women, hunting game and fish, naked, illiterate, and innumerate.

In the first century of settlement, it became clear that it was difficult to use Indians as slave labor. They were not docile, had a high mortality rate when exposed to Western diseases, and could run away and hide rather easily. Portugal turned to imported African slaves for manual labor. The ultimate fate of the indigenous population was rather like that in North America. They were pushed beyond the fringe of colonial society.

In the sixteenth and seventeenth centuries, Portuguese gains from Brazil came from plantation agriculture, commodity exports, and commercial profit. A small settler population controlled highly profitable export-oriented sugar plantations in the Northeast. Their techniques, using slave labor, followed the pattern the Portuguese had developed at São Tomé in Africa. Cattle ranching in the dry backlands area provided food for those working in sugar production. Official revenue from Brazil was rather small, about 3 percent of Portuguese public revenue in 1588 and 5 percent in 1619; at that time, Asia provided ten times as much (see Bethell, 1984, vol.1, p. 286).

Portuguese trade with Brazil was much less rigidly organized than that of Spain with its colonies. There was less state interference and greater scope for participation by other European countries. There was a significant Brazilian-owned merchant marine engaged in coastal shipping and the slave trade with Africa (see Klein 1999, 36). The governance of the colony was less tightly controlled, and the ecclesiastical regime was more tolerant. In 1640, when Portugal regained independence from Spain, it allied itself closely with Britain. The British were allowed to have merchants in Brazil and Portugal and to engage in the carrying trade. In return, the British propped up the Portuguese empire with military guarantees.

Brazilian sugar exports peaked in the 1650s. Earnings fell thereafter because of lower prices and competition from the rapidly growing output in the Caribbean. The setback in sugar caused large parts of the Northeast to lapse into a subsistence economy. In the 1690s, the discovery of gold and, in the 1720s, diamonds in Minas Gerais opened new opportunities. During the eighteenth century, there was considerable immigration from Europe, and internal migration from the Northeast to Minas, to engage in gold and diamond development. Eighteenth-century prosperity in Minas is obvious even today from the number of elaborate buildings and churches in Ouro Prêto, the center of mining activity. As Minas is very barren, the food and transport needs of the mining area stimulated food production in neighboring provinces to the South and in the Northeast and mule breeding in Rio Grande do Sul. The gold industry peaked around 1750, with production around fifteen tons a year, but as the best deposits were exhausted, output and exports declined. In the first half of the eighteenth century, identifiable royal revenues from the gold trade were around 18 percent of Portuguese government revenue. Total Brazilian gold shipments over the whole of the eighteenth century were between 800 and 850 tons.

In the second half of the eighteenth century, Portuguese finances were in desperate straits. Revenues from Brazil were squeezed by the decline in gold production. Income from Asia had collapsed, and Portugal had to bear the costs of reconstructing Lisbon after the 1755 earthquake. To meet this problem, Pombal, the Portuguese prime minister, expelled the Jesuits from Brazil (in 1759), confiscated their vast properties, and sold them to wealthy landowners and merchants for the benefit of the crown. Most of the property of other religious orders was taken over a few years later.

When gold production collapsed, Brazil returned to agricultural exports. At independence in 1822, the three main exports were cotton, sugar, and coffee.

At the end of the colonial period, half of the population were slaves. They were fed on a crude diet of beans and jerked beef and worked to death after a few years of service. A privileged fraction of the white population enjoyed high incomes, but the rest of the population (indigenous, free blacks, mulattoes, and a large number of whites) were poor. Landownership was concentrated on slave owners; thus a very unequal distribution of property buttressed a highly unequal distribution of income. There was also substantial regional inequality. The poorest area was the Northeast, and Minas had passed its peak. The most prosperous area was around the new capital, Rio de Janeiro.

Independence came to Brazil very smoothly by Latin American standards. In 1808, the Portuguese queen and the regent fled to Rio to escape the French invasion. They brought 10,000 people with them—the aristocracy, bureaucracy, and some of the military. They set up their government and court in Rio and Petropolis, running Brazil and Portugal as a joint kingdom. After the Napoleonic wars, the two countries split without too much enmity. Brazil became independent with an emperor who was the son of the Portuguese monarch. This regime changed in 1888–89 with the abolition of slavery and establishment of a republic (see figure 2b on the comparative economic performance of Brazil and the United States, 1700–2001).

Characteristics of Dutch, British, and French Colonialism in the Caribbean

The Caribbean was the initial locus of Spanish activity in the Americas but was neglected after the discovery of silver in Peru and Mexico and the virtual extinction of the indigenous population. For two centuries thereafter, Spain used the Caribbean mainly as a base for its treasure fleets. The Caribbean became a center of activity for Dutch, British, and French corsairs (officially sanctioned raiders and pirates), who successfully sacked Havana, Maracaibo, Portobello, Trinidad, and Veracruz and captured a large number of Spanish treasure ships. Because of this piracy, Spain adopted a convoy system for its trade with the Americas.

The British took the uninhabited island of Barbados in 1627, intending to produce food and tobacco with indentured white immigrants. A little later the French took Guadeloupe, Martinique, and six other islands with similar intentions. In the 1620s, the Dutch occupied the Northeast of Brazil (during the period when

Spain had taken over Portugal). They were expelled in 1654 and moved to Barbados, Guadeloupe, and Martinique, demonstrating the profitability of sugar production, by providing technical assistance, machinery, shipping, marketing facilities, and slaves. The British and French colonies were quickly transformed. Henceforth, they concentrated almost exclusively on sugar and relied on imports for most of their food. Tobacco cultivation and white immigration dwindled rapidly. After the Dutch had served their purpose, they were expelled.[7]

The French and British ran their colonies on a mutually exclusive basis. They could sell only to their respective metropoles and their colonies (though there were substantial reexports from England and France to foreign markets). A similar pattern of exclusivity applied to imports. The food imports of the British colonies came mainly from England; timber and other supplies came from New England. The French and British took over most of the slave trade to the Caribbean. Sugar refining was done mainly in the metropoles.

Sugar proved so profitable that the British seized Jamaica from Spain in 1655. The French gained a footing in the western part of Hispaniola, which became their colony of St. Domingue in 1697. These two large islands became the biggest producers in the Caribbean. The Spanish were left with Cuba, Puerto Rico, the eastern half of Hispaniola (lost to France in 1795), and Trinidad (lost to Britain in 1803). Until the second half of the eighteenth century, Spanish sugar production was quite small. It started to expand rapidly after the British occupation of Havana in 1762–63. By 1787, Cuba was exporting fifty-six kilograms per head of population. During the War of American Independence, Cuban exports replaced the sugar and rum that British colonies had shipped to North America.

Caribbean sugar production rose about tenfold between the 1660s and the 1780s. By 1787, sugar exports of the nineteen British West Indian colonies averaged 195 kilograms per head; exports of French colonies averaged 240 kilograms.

Sugar plantations were large enterprises requiring substantial capital investment. As the labor force was made up of slaves, there was extreme income inequality in the islands. The profits were siphoned off to absentee owners, who preferred the healthier climate of their home country.

The Caribbean lobby of sugar planters and slave traders was very powerful socially and politically in the United Kingdom. In 1661, Charles II created thirteen baronets with interests in Barbados. Planters and slavers were also well represented in the House of Commons. Absentee owners educated their children in England. There was only one secondary school in Barbados and another in Jamaica and no provision for higher education. Codrington, a planter on the Leeward Islands, gave his books to the library he financed in All Souls College, Oxford. The Lascelles family from Barbados later married into British royalty. William Beckford had an imposing country seat in Wiltshire, became lord mayor of London, and, in 1763, after the war with France, persuaded his friend the prime minister (Chatham) to give Guadeloupe back to France, as its acquisition would have established an unwelcome competitor in the protected British sugar market (see Williams 1970, 114, 132).

During the Napoleonic wars, French interests in the Caribbean suffered greatly from interruptions in trade and the slave revolt in Haiti, which became independent in 1804. French sugar shipments from the Caribbean were 70 percent lower in 1815 than in 1787 and never recovered their previous level again, partly because of the development and protection of beet sugar production in France.

Britain abolished the slave trade in 1807 and slavery in 1833, with £20 million compensation for the slave owners and nothing for the slaves. Abolition was due in substantial part to the success of humanitarian reformers in convincing public opinion to end a repugnant form of exploitation. The loss of privileged export markets in North America after 1776 and the successful slave revolt in Haiti persuaded the planting lobby that their days were numbered and that it was in their interest to settle for compensation. France abolished the slave trade in 1817 and slavery in 1848. The Dutch abolished slavery in 1863.

The end of slavery raised costs and weakened the competitive position of most Caribbean producers (in spite of the introduction of

700,000 indentured Asian workers between 1838 and 1913). In 1787, the Caribbean had accounted for 90 percent of world sugar exports. By 1913, its share had fallen to a sixth. There was diversification in favor of coffee and cotton, but the main impact was stagnant or falling income. Eisner (1961, 119, 153) estimated that per capita real income in Jamaica fell by a quarter between 1832 and 1870 and exports from 41 to 15 percent of GDP; by 1930, the per capita GDP level was about the same as in 1832! For the British and French islands, this experience was probably fairly typical. However, Spain retained slavery in Cuba and Puerto Rico until 1886 and was successful in expanding and modernizing sugar production; exports rose from 30,000 tons in 1787 to 2.8 million in 1913.

In the nineteenth century, there was a precipitate fall in the relative importance of Caribbean trade. In 1774, the Caribbean provided 29 percent of total British imports but by 1913 less than 1 percent. The collapse in French imports was equally dramatic. By contrast, British imports from North America rose from 12.5 percent of the total in 1774 to 22.6 percent in 1913.

In the eighteenth century, the Caribbean was the most profitable area of European colonization in the Americas. By 1870, it was an impoverished backwater.

British North America

The economy and social structure of North America were very different from those in the Caribbean, Brazil, or the Spanish viceroyalties.

In the northern colonies, slaves were less than 5 percent of the population. A large part of the predominantly white labor force were farmers working their own land. The average family farm in New England, the mid-Atlantic states, and Pennsylvania in 1807 had well over one hundred acres (Lebergott 1984, 17). Per capita income was about the same as in the United Kingdom and more evenly distributed.

Most of the northern colonies had been formed by Protestants of various denominations who were keen on education. There were eight universities in the North (Harvard, founded in 1636; Yale, 1701; University of Pennsylvania, 1740; Princeton, 1746; Columbia, 1754; Brown, 1764; Rutgers, 1766; Dartmouth, 1769), and one (William and Mary, 1693) in the South. The level of education in the northern colonies was above that in the United Kingdom.

In 1820, the states that relied most heavily on slave labor (Maryland, Virginia, the Carolinas, and Georgia) contained about 30 percent of the U.S. population. About 40 percent of the population in these states were slaves, compared with 85 percent in the Caribbean. Whites (indentured servants and others) were a significant part of the labor force. The main plantation crops were tobacco, rice, and indigo, where work intensity was less than in sugar. The climate was healthier than in the Caribbean. Life expectancy and possibilities for natural growth of the black population were greater. Growth of the labor force depended much less on the slave trade.

Although the British Navigation Acts had made the colonies route most of their trade with Europe through Britain, they provided favored access to markets within the empire. These were particularly important for exports of foodstuffs, shipping services, and ships. On the eve of the War of American Independence, the merchant marine of the colonies was over 450,000 tons, all of which (coastal craft, West Indies schooners, fishing and whaling boats, and ships for trade with England) was built in New England shipyards with easy access to cheap timber, pitch, and tar. American shipyards built an increasing proportion of the British merchant fleet in the course of the eighteenth century. In 1774, 30 percent was American built.

The North American colonies had a significant urban population in Boston, New York, and Philadelphia. They had a politically sophisticated elite familiar with the ideas and ideals of the French enlightenment. Their incentive to break the colonial tie was reinforced in 1763, after the Seven Years War, in which the British ended French rule in Canada and French claims to territory west of the thirteen colonies. Hitherto, the most likely alternative to British rule had been French rule; thereafter, it was independence.

A striking characteristic of U.S. economic growth after independence was its much greater dynamism than that of its neighbor Mexico, which was a Spanish colony until 1825. It is, therefore, useful to compare the different institutional, societal, and policy influences transmitted by Spain and the United Kingdom.

The main reasons for Mexican backwardness compared with the ex-British colonies in North America were probably as follows:

1. The Spanish colony was subject to a bigger drain of resources. A considerable part of domestic income went into the pockets of peninsular Spaniards, who took their savings back home. Official tribute took another 2.7 percent of GDP (see Maddison 1995b, 316–17).

2. The British colonial regime imposed mercantilist restrictions on foreign trade, but they were much lighter than in New Spain. Thomas (1965) suggested that the net cost of British trade restrictions was about 42 cents per head in the American colonies in 1770 (about 0.6 percent of GDP).

3. The British colonists had better education, greater intellectual freedom, and social mobility. Education was secular, with emphasis on pragmatic skills and Yankee ingenuity, of which Ben Franklin was the prototype. New Spain had only two universities (in Mexico City and Guadalajara), both of which concentrated on theology and law. Throughout the colonial period, the Inquisition maintained a tight censorship and suppressed heterodox thinking.

4. In New Spain, the best land was controlled by hacienda owners. In North America, the white population had much easier access to land, and in New England, family farming enterprise was typical. Restricted access to land in the Spanish colonies was recognized as a hindrance to economic growth by both Adam Smith and the viceroy

of New Spain. Rosenzweig (1963) quotes the latter as follows (my translation): "Maldistribution of land is a major obstacle to the progress of agriculture and commerce, particularly with regard to entails with absentee or negligent owners. We have subjects of his majesty here who possess hundreds of square leagues—enough to form a small kingdom—but who produce little of value."

5. New Spain had a privileged upper class, with a sumptuary lifestyle. Differences in status—a hereditary aristocracy, privileged groups of clergy and military with tax exemptions, and legal immunities—meant that there was much less entrepreneurial vigor than in the British colonies. The elite in New Spain were rent seekers with a low propensity for productive investment.

6. In the government of New Spain, power was highly concentrated, whereas in British North America, there were thirteen separate colonies. Political power was fragmented, so there was much greater freedom for individuals to pursue their own economic interests.

7. Another source of advantage for North America was the vigor of its population growth because of the rapid inflow of migrants. The population of the thirteen colonies rose tenfold from 1700 to 1820 and by less than half in Mexico. Economic enterprise was much more dynamic when the market was expanding so rapidly.

FIGURE 2A

COMPARATIVE LEVELS OF MEXICAN AND U.S. GDP PER CAPITA, 1700–2001

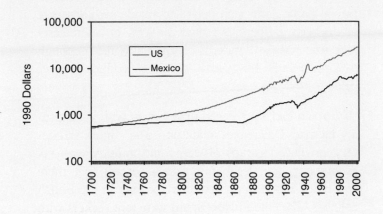

SOURCE: Maddison (2003).

FIGURE 2B

COMPARATIVE LEVELS OF BRAZILIAN AND U.S. GDP PER CAPITA, 1700–2001

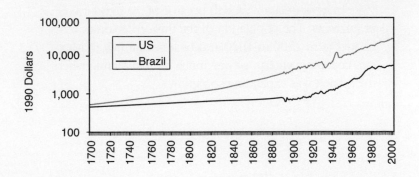

SOURCE: Maddison (2003).

PART III

The Interaction between Asia and Europe, 1500–1820

The European impact was much more modest in Asia than in the Americas. The population of Asia was five times as big as that of Western Europe in 1500. The technological level was sophisticated, and the capacity of major states such as the Mogul Empire, China, or Japan to resist conquest by European countries was clear. Asian destinations were more remote, with a sailing time measured in months rather than weeks.

The Advent of the Europeans

The Portuguese pioneered direct trade links with Asia at the end of the fifteenth century. The initiative came from the crown. Their trading empire consisted of armed ships and a string of fortified island bases: Elmina and Mozambique on the African coast, Hormuz at the entry to the Persian Gulf, Goa on the northwest coast of India (the headquarters of Asian trading operations and the Jesuit order). Malacca controlled trade and shipping between India and Indonesia, and Macao was the main locus of trade with China. There were also important trading posts at Jaffna in Ceylon, Nagasaki in Japan, and Ternate in the Moluccas.

Portuguese exports from Asia to Europe were heavily concentrated on spices. Initially, they were financed by bullion shipments, as Asians had little interest in European goods. An increasing proportion were financed from fees levied on Asian traders using ports controlled by Portugal and earnings in intra-Asian trade. The most lucrative were their sales of Chinese silks and other Asian goods for 3,000 tons of Japanese silver between the 1550s and 1639.

Portuguese penetration of the Asian oceans was facilitated by the withdrawal of China and Japan from international trade. At the beginning of the fifteenth century, Chinese naval technology was superior to that of Europe. Chinese fleets were deployed in spectacular voyages throughout the Indian Ocean and down the East African coast from 1405 to 1433. Thereafter, China concentrated on internal trade via the reconstructed Grand Canal and more or less abandoned international trade and construction of sophisticated ships. From 1639 to the middle of the nineteenth century, the Tokugawa regime restricted Japan's foreign contacts to a small Dutch trading settlement at Deshima, near Nagasaki.

When the Portuguese arrived in the Indian Ocean, there was no powerful naval force to oppose them. They were attacked by an Egyptian fleet in 1509, but it was decisively defeated at Diu off the coast of Gujarat. The Asian traders with whom the Portuguese were competing belonged to merchant communities (with varying ethnic, religious, family, or linguistic ties), operating without armed vessels or significant interference from governments. Although southern India, where Portugal started its Asian trade, was ruled by the Empire of Vijayanagar, conditions in coastal trade were set by rulers of small political units, who derived income by offering protection and marketing opportunities. The income of the rulers of Vijayanagar and the Mogul Empire was derived from land taxes, and they had no significant financial interest in foreign trade. In Indonesia, political power was fragmented; the Hindu state of Majapahit was in decline and uninterested in foreign trade. In China and Japan, the situation was different, and the Portuguese had to negotiate a limited entry, cap in hand.

Portuguese trade in Asia declined in the seventeenth century. There was competition from the revival of the old spice route to Europe via Egypt. At the beginning of the century, the Dutch captured Malacca and Jaffna and took over the trade monopoly with

Japan. Dutch competition weakened Portuguese interests in Bengal and on the west coast of India. Portugal lost its bases at Hormuz in 1622 and Muscat in 1650. Nevertheless, Goa and Macao were retained for more than 400 years. Portugal compensated for its Asian losses by developing an empire in Brazil.

The total volume of European shipping in Asian waters was four times as big in the seventeenth and nine times as big in the eighteenth as it had been in the sixteenth century. Portugal became a marginal participant, with about 12 percent of the trade in the seventeenth and 3 percent in the eighteenth century. The Dutch accounted for half of the expanded trade, the British about a quarter. French and three small European companies (Danish, Swedish, and Ostend) accounted for the rest.

The European market for traditional exports of pepper and spices was limited. The bulk of the new export items was raw silk, a huge variety of cotton textiles from India, coffee from Arabia and Indonesia, and tea from China.

The Dutch Company (VOC) accounted for 45 percent of the European voyages to Asia from 1500 to 1800 and a higher proportion of the tonnage. It was given a monopoly charter (in 1602), which it needed to organize a trade with heavy capital outlays over extended periods. Each 30,000-mile round-trip voyage to its Asian headquarters in Java (Batavia) took at least eighteen months. Dutch ships were armed, and the company had the power to wage war, make treaties with Asian rulers, establish fortified ports, and enlist soldiers and administrators.

The company had six shipyards in the Netherlands and maintained a fleet of about one hundred vessels. The average vessel was replaced after ten years, during which it would have made four round trips to Asia. Over the lifetime of the company, 1,500 ships were constructed for the Asian trade. At the end of the sixteenth century, the Portuguese were using large carracks with an average size well over 1,000 tons. The Dutch started with ships below 500 tons. By the 1770s, the average was about 1,000 tons, which was bigger than vessels used by the English and French companies. Dutch losses from shipwreck and seizure were below 3 percent over the whole period 1600–1800, which was very much smaller than the Portuguese experienced.

By 1750, the company employed more than 12,000 sailors and 17,000 soldiers as well as its administrative personnel in Asia. Over the whole period 1600–1800, the VOC sent nearly a million sailors, soldiers, and administrators to its thirty Asian trading posts. This was about the same as the combined total for other European companies (British, French, Portuguese, Danish, Swedish, and Austria's Ostend Company). The proportion of the Dutch Company's servants who returned to Europe (about a third) was a good deal lower than that of other companies. This was due to the greater role of intra-Asian trade in the VOC's operations and the bigger proportion of VOC personnel who stayed in Asia permanently, but it seems likely that the mortality rate was higher. Over the course of the eighteenth century, the incidence of malaria rose dramatically in Batavia as the area of swampland around the city increased.

After the British took over the governance of Bengal in 1757, discrimination against Dutch operations weakened VOC trade with India. Its position in China trade was also greatly inferior to the British, who used opium shipments from India to finance their tea purchases in Canton, whereas the Dutch had to pay in bullion for tea delivered by Chinese traders to Batavia. The outbreak of the Napoleonic wars led to a British takeover of Dutch interests in India, Malacca, Ceylon, South Africa, and temporarily in Indonesia.

In the second half of the eighteenth century, the VOC had ceased to be a profitable organization. It collapsed into bankruptcy in 1795, after several decades of distributing dividends bigger than its profits. The profit decline was largely due to the very high overhead of the company in hiring military, naval, and administrative personnel to run what had become a territorial empire in Java and Ceylon. The officers of the VOC conducted an increasingly large private trade in the company's ships. There was also a good deal of corruption in the administration of Java and Ceylon, which benefited the servants but not the shareholders of the company. Given the changing commodity structure of trade and the locus of operation, Batavia was no longer the ideal headquarters it had been initially, when the spice trade was predominant.

The Impact of Asian Trade on Europe

Asian trade stimulated expansion of the European shipping industry and improvement of navigation techniques. It created new employment opportunities and provided new kinds of consumer goods for which demand was highly elastic. Tea and coffee improved social life. To the degree that they replaced gin and beer, they increased life expectancy. Asian textiles and porcelain created new fashions in clothing, domestic utensils, decorative fabrics, and wallpaper. Familiarity with these new goods eventually sparked European import substitution, particularly in textiles, pottery, and porcelain.

The most striking thing about the operation of European companies from 1500 to 1800 was not their exploitation of Asia but their enmity to each other. This was most extreme in relations between the Portuguese and the Dutch, but it was also visible in British-Dutch and British-French action and attitudes. Apart from the cost of armed struggles, there were heavy military commitments to deter conflict, monopolistic interdiction of European markets to competitors, and creation of separate networks of trading posts. All of this raised the costs and reduced the benefits of trade to Europeans as well as Asians. It contrasted unfavorably with conditions in the trading world of Asia before European entrance and the widespread acceptance of a free-trade regime between the 1840s and 1913.

The Impact of Europe on Asia

European trading posts in Asia were nearly all on the coastal periphery, and until the eighteenth century, infringements of Asian sovereignty were generally limited. In the second half of the century, a major change occurred when Britain took over the administration and revenues of part of the collapsing Mogul Empire. In Indonesia, the Dutch achieved monopoly control of the Spice Islands early in the seventeenth century by slaughtering the inhabitants and installing new plantations operated by slave labor. Elsewhere in Indonesia there was a lesser degree of coercion until after the Napoleonic wars. Europeans posed no challenge to Chinese or Japanese sovereignty until the nineteenth century.

The European companies created new markets in Europe for Asian products. Prakash (1998, 317), estimates that British and Dutch purchases of textiles accounted for about 11 percent of textile employment in Bengal in the period 1678–1718. The East India Company (EIC) also created new towns as centers of commerce in Bombay, Calcutta, and Madras. There was relatively little demand for European goods in Asia. European purchases were financed by transfer of precious metals or earnings from intra-Asian trade. However, the export of silver to India and China did help to monetize their economies. The most obvious adverse economic impact of the European companies on Asia was to displace the shipping and marketing activities of Asian traders.

After 1757, when the EIC took over the governance of Bengal, the British relationship with India, became exploitative, as exports to Britain and opium exports to China were financed out of the tax revenue from Bengal.

There is not much evidence of significant transfer of European technology to Asia. To understand why, it is useful to scrutinize the experience of China and India, as they accounted for three-quarters of the Asian population and GDP in 1500.

Chinese Characteristics Affecting Economic Performance

China was by far the most powerful and technologically advanced country in Asia. Printed books with extensive illustrations were available five centuries earlier than in Europe. The highly literate, secular Chinese elite had a worldview unconstrained by the religious dogma that handicapped intellectual advance in Europe before the fifteenth century, when the literate population were mostly priests. The difference is clear in the fundamental area of astronomy. Chinese ideas of time and space were closer to those of Galileo than to the pre-Copernican orthodoxy of Europe. Chinese medieval cosmology was "far more modern than that of Europe, for instead of crystalline celestial spheres they thought in terms of infinite empty space and an almost infinitude of time. The Chinese were the most persistent and accurate observers of celestial phenomena in any culture before the Renaissance. . . . The Bureau of Astronomy was an integral part of the civil service and the Bureau of Historiography could be relied upon to hand the records down. Thus the first Chinese eclipse records date as far back as 1361 BC" (Needham 1970, 2–3, 398).

The economic impact of the bureaucracy was generally very positive in agriculture. Their policies were successful in sustaining "extensive" growth. Over the period 1000–1820, agricultural output kept up with a population growth much faster than that in any other part of Asia and faster than in Western Europe. They thought of agriculture as the key sector from which they could squeeze a surplus in the form of taxes and levies. They helped develop and diffuse new seeds and crops. Best-practice techniques were diffused by commissioning and distributing agricultural handbooks and calendars. They ensured that the advice they contained was adopted by selected farmers in different regions. Bray (1984) cites extensive bibliographies that show the existence of more than 500 (mostly official) works on agriculture (78 pre-Sung, 105 Sung, 26 Yuan, and 310 Ming-Ching texts). From the tenth century, they were available in printed form. Ho (1959) shows when new world plants were introduced in China; the peanut was probably the first, being introduced by the Portuguese in 1516, the sweet potato was first recorded in local histories in the 1560s, maize in 1574, and the potato in the seventeenth century.

The exceptional burst of "intensive" growth (sustaining a rise of a third in per capita income) that China achieved in the Sung dynasty stemmed essentially from agriculture. There was a major shift toward double-cropped irrigated rice in South China and a concomitant shift in the center of gravity of the population from the North to the area south of the Yangtze.

Outside agriculture, it is clear that the bureaucratic system had negative effects. The bureaucracy and the associated gentry were quintessential rent-seekers. They prevented the emergence of an independent commercial and industrial bourgeoisie on the European pattern. Entrepreneurial activity was insecure in a framework where legal protection for private activity was exiguous. Any activity that promised to be lucrative was subject to bureaucratic squeeze. The most striking example of the adverse effect of bureaucratic regulation was the virtual closure of China to international trade early in the fifteenth century and the subsequent disappearance of its sophisticated shipbuilding industry.

Needham (1981) argued that China never developed "the fundamental bases of modern science, such as the application of mathematical hypotheses to Nature, the full understanding and use of the experimental method and the systematic accumulation of openly published scientific data." Lin (1995) made essentially the same point. China, in spite of its early sophistication, fell behind the West because it "did not make the shift from experience-based to experiment cum science-based innovation, while Europe did so through the scientific revolution in the seventeenth century."

China took a disdainful attitude toward Western technology before the twentieth century. The bureaucracy was ethnocentric, indifferent to developments outside China. Jesuit scholars had been in Peking for nearly two centuries; some of them like Ricci, Schall, and Verbiest had intimate contact with ruling circles, but there was little curiosity about the West. In an unsuccessful attempt to open diplomatic relations, Lord Macartney spent a year, in 1792–93, transporting 600 cases of presents from George III. They included a planetarium, globes, mathematical instruments, chronometers, a telescope, measuring instruments, plate glass, copperware, chemicals, and other miscellaneous items. After he presented them to the Ch'ien-lung emperor in Jehol, the official response stated: "There is nothing we lack. We have never set much store on strange or ingenious objects, nor do we need any more of your country's manufactures." (Teng and Fairbank 1954).

Indian Characteristics Affecting Economic Performance

India was very different from China. It had many ethnic and religious divisions, and no common language or printed books. Education was not secular but religious for both Muslims and Hindus. Governance of the Mogul empire was provided by a predatory aristocracy of Muslim warlords, who were able to squeeze a large fiscal surplus (land tax revenue) from a docile rural population (mostly Hindus). Villages were defensive, self-contained units designed for survival in periods of war and alien domination. Villagers paid taxes collectively to whoever held state power. Conquerors of India had a ready source of income and no incentive to change the system.

The docility of village society derived from the caste system, which segregated the population into mutually exclusive groups whose functions were hereditary. There were four groups. Brahmins were at the top of the social scale. Their priestly purity was not to be polluted by manual labor. Next in rank came warriors (*kshatriyas*), traders (*vaishyas*), and farm workers (*sudras*). Below were outcastes, who performed menial and unclean tasks. This system had an adverse effect on productivity because it pushed village living standards to a level that reduced physical working capacity, allocated jobs on a rigid basis of heredity rather than aptitude, promoted a ritualistic rather than a functional attitude to work, and maintained taboos on animal slaughter.

As a result the Indian economy was characterized by long-term stagnation and negligible levels of productive investment. The irrigated area was about 5 percent of the total, compared with a third in China. Animal dung was rarely used as manure, and a largely vegetarian population got little benefit from large numbers of sacred cows. There were no agricultural handbooks or state attempts to bolster agricultural productivity. Crop yields seem to have been stagnant over the long run. Demographic expansion was much slower than in China from 1500 to 1820.

One of the most significant differences between China and India was the availability of land. The area suitable for cultivation was much greater in relation to the population in India than in China.

An economy with relatively abundant land is more likely to use coercive institutions (like the caste system or slavery) than China, where land was much scarcer and rural property relationships were very different.

The income the Mogul elite, native princes, and *zamindars* (Hindu nobles with hereditary control of village revenues) managed to squeeze from the rural population was proportionately quite large. It amounted to about 15 percent of the national income, about double the proportion going to the Chinese imperial household, bureaucracy, and gentry (see Maddison 1971). The Mogul elite and the urban population were the main beneficiaries. The emperor built magnificent palaces and mosques at Agra, Delhi, Fatehpur Sikri, and Lahore. The nobility lived in walled castles with harems, gardens, and fountains. They maintained polygamous households with large retinues of servants and slaves. They had huge wardrobes of splendid garments in fine cottons and silk.

Mogul officials were not landlords but were allocated tax revenue for a specified area (*jagir*). They were regularly posted from one *jagir* to another, and their estates were subject to royal forfeit on death. There was little incentive to improve landed property. The *jagirdar* had an incentive to squeeze village society close to subsistence, spend lavishly on consumption, and die in debt to the state.

Economic activity in urban areas went to meet the demands of the elite. Handicraft industries produced high-quality cotton textiles, silks, jewelry, decorative swords, and weapons. There was plenty of scope for petty traders, merchants, and bankers. A large force of construction workers built the palaces and mosques. The majority of urban dwellers were Muslims. Compared to village society, their tax burden was light.

European contact with India was much more extensive than with China from the sixteenth to the early nineteenth century, but transfer of technology was mainly to, rather than from, Europe. In most cases, European companies in India were not directly involved in productive activity. Their orders for Indian goods went through Indian merchants and brokers, so they had little influence on techniques of production. Habib (1978–79) and Qaisar (1982) provide a useful synopsis of the state of Indian technology from 1500 to 1700 and describe the fields in which technology transfer occurred.

The Jesuits brought a printing press to Goa and started operating it in 1556. They presented a polyglot Bible to the Emperor Akbar in 1580 but did not succeed in arousing much curiosity. The English East India Company brought a printer to Surat in 1675, but he was not able to cast type in Indian scripts, so the venture failed. Printing was not considered seriously by the aristocratic patrons of Indian scribes and manuscript illuminators.

There was an interest in European handguns, muskets, and artillery. Indian rulers employed European technicians in this field, and Indian artisans were quite adept at copying and developing many items. However, Indian troops seldom acquired weaponry equivalent to the European. Their gunsmiths did not succeed in casting iron suitable for artillery pieces, which continued to be cast in bronze.

The Portuguese built ships of European design in India for sale to local merchants. The British built ships in Surat for use by the East India Company, and English ships' carpenters seem to have transmitted their knowledge to Indian artisans. However, they had little serious impact on traditional Indian ship design. India already had astrolabes and other navigational devices and made little attempt to copy European instruments.

Land transport was unaffected by European technology before the introduction of railways. Bullocks remained the basic draught animal. Horses were not used for carts and carriages. India did not replicate the horse harness developed in Europe in the tenth century and in China much earlier. The wheelbarrow had been invented in China in the third century and in the twelfth in Europe, but long after the contact with Europe, India continued to move loads by head or hod. The Indian glass industry seems to have been immune to European technology. Lanterns, mirrors, telescopes, and eyeglasses were "foreign curiosities and rarities," not produced in India. The Indians, like the Chinese, made no attempt to replicate European clocks.

There was some transfer of New World crops. Tobacco arrived after 1600. Its cultivation developed rather quickly and extensively. Maize was introduced in the seventeenth century but was not widely diffused. There was more enthusiasm for pineapples, which arrived at the same time.

PART IV

The Contours of African Development

The long-term economic development of Africa is difficult to quantify with any precision. However, it is possible to discern the broad contours of population growth, and there are some clues on the development of per capita income.

There was a marked difference between experience north of the Sahara and on the rest of the continent. For most of the past two millennia, income and urbanization levels were higher, and economic and political institutions more sophisticated, in the North than in the South. North African history is reasonably well documented, because there are substantial written records. Knowledge of the South is based on archaeological or linguistic evidence until the ninth century, when written evidence of northern visitors becomes available. Over the long run, population growth was much more dynamic south of the Sahara. Two thousand years ago, about half of all Africans lived in the North; by 1820, four-fifths lived in the South. Between the first century AD and 1820, the population of the North increased by a third (with many intervening setbacks). In the rest of Africa, it increased nearly eightfold (see table 9). In terms of extensive growth (i.e., capacity to accommodate population increase), the South clearly had the edge. In terms of per capita real income, it seems likely that the average northern level was lower in 1820 than in the first century. South of the Sahara, it probably increased modestly (see table 10).

The greater demographic dynamism of the South is surprising because of its substantial losses from the slave trade. There seem to be three reasons for this:

TABLE 9
AFRICAN POPULATION, 1–2001 AD
(thousands)

	1	1000	1500	1600	1700	1820	2001
Egypt	4,000	5,000	4,000	5,000	4,500	4,194	71,902
Morocco	1,000	2,000	1,500	2,250	1,750	2,689	30,645
Algeria	2,000	2,000	1,500	2,250	1,750	2,689	31,736
Tunisia	800	1,000	800	1,000	800	875	9,705
Libya	400	500	500	500	500	538	5,241
Total North Africa	8,200	10,500	8,300	11,000	9,300	10,985	149,229
Sahel	1,000	2,000	3,000	3,500	4,000	4,887	32,885
Other West Africa	3,000	7,000	11,000	14,000	18,000	20,777	218,393
Total West Africa	4,000	9,000	14,000	17,500	22,000	25,664	251,278
Ethiopia and Eritrea	500	1,000	2,000	2,250	2,500	3,154	68,208
Sudan	2,000	3,000	4,000	4,200	4,400	5,156	36,080
Somalia	200	400	800	800	950	1,000	7,489
Other East Africa	300	3,000	6,000	7,000	8,000	10,389	103,338
Total East Africa	3,000	7,400	12,800	14,250	15,850	19,699	215,115
Angola, Zaire, Equatoria	1,000	4,000	8,000	8,500	9,000	10,757	87,235
Malawi, Zambia, Zimbabwe	75	500	1,000	1,100	1,200	1,345	33,452
Mozambique	50	300	1,000	1,250	1,500	2,096	17,142
South Africa, Swaziland, Lesotho	100	300	600	700	1,000	1,550	45,562
Namibia and Botswana	75	100	200	200	200	219	3,444
Madagascar	0	200	700	800	1,000	1,683	15,983
Indian Ocean	0	0	10	20	30	238	2,648
Total Southern Africa	300	1,400	3,510	4,070	4,930	7,131	118,231
Total Africa	16,500	32,300	46,610	55,320	61,080	74,236	821,088

SOURCE: Maddison (2003a, 190). *Sahel* includes Chad, Mauritania, Mali, and Niger. *Other West Africa* includes Senegal, Gambia, Guinea Bissau, Guinea, Sierra Leone, Liberia, Burkina Faso, Ivory Coast, Ghana, Togo, Benin, Nigeria, Cape Verde, and Western Sahara. *Equatoria* includes Cameroon, Central African Republic, Congo, Equatorial Guinea, Gabon, and São Tomé and Principe. *Indian Ocean* includes Comoros, Mauritius, Mayotte, Réunion, and Seychelles. *Other East Africa* includes Burundi, Djibouti, Kenya, Rwanda, Tanzania, and Uganda.

THE CONTOURS OF AFRICAN DEVELOPMENT 69

TABLE 10

AFRICAN GDP PER CAPITA, 1–2001

(1990 international dollars)

	1	1000	1500	1600	1700	1820	2001
Egypt	500	500	475	475	475	475	2,992
Morocco	400	430	430	430	430	430	2,782
Other North Africa	430	430	430	430	430	430	3,148
Sahel and West Africa	400	415	415	415	415	415	1,058
Rest of Africa	400	400	400	415	415	415	1,211
Average	430	425	414	422	421	420	1,489

SOURCE: Maddison (2003a, 191) for 1–1820, for which the figures are stylized conjectures. Estimates for 2001 and movement 1820–2001 as described in Maddison (2003a, 197–201). The rationale for the conjectures derives from the analysis of the main currents in African history. In the first century AD, North Africa belonged to the Roman Empire. Egypt was the richest part because of the special character of its agriculture, which had yielded a large surplus for governance and monuments in Pharaonic times and was generally siphoned off as tribute by Roman and Arab rulers. Libya and most of the Maghreb (except Morocco) had a prosperous, urbanized coastal fringe, with Berber tribes between them and the Sahara. There was no contact then with black Africa, which I assume had an average income only slightly above subsistence ($400 in my numéraire). After the Arab conquest of North Africa in the seventh century, camel transport opened trade across the Sahara, permitting a rise in per capita income in Morocco, the Sahel, and West Africa. I assume that the gradual transition within black Africa from a hunter-gatherer to an agricultural mode of production led to increased density of settlement with higher per capita labor inputs but had little impact on per capita income.

1. In Egypt and the Maghreb, plague seems to have been endemic from the sixth to the early nineteenth century. It does not seem to have crossed the Sahara.

2. Before the eighth century, there was virtually no contact between North and South. Possibilities for trade across the Sahara were revolutionized by the introduction of camels between the fifth and eighth centuries. They could carry about a third of a ton of freight, go without food for several days, and go without water for up to fifteen days. The partial Islamization of black Africa increased the sophistication and organizational ability

of the ruling elites in the Sahel and savannah lands of West Africa south of the Sahara.

3. Probably the most important factor was the spread of improved agricultural technology and new crops. Two thousand years ago, much of black Africa was inhabited by hunter-gatherers using stone-age technology. By 1820, they had been pushed aside and were a fraction of the population. The proportion of agriculturalists and pastoralists with Iron Age tools and weapons increased dramatically. Land productivity was also helped by the introduction and gradual diffusion of maize, cassava, and sweet potatoes from the Americas from 1500 onward.

Egypt

In the first century AD, all of North Africa was under Roman rule. The Mediterranean was a Roman lake with magnificent ports in Italy and Alexandria and substantial flows of trade between Africa, Europe, and the Middle East. Egypt was the most prosperous area, with a relatively large urban population, a sedentary agriculture, a substantially monetized economy, a significant industrial and commercial sector, and a very long history as an organized state. Its natural waterways lowered the cost of transporting freight and passengers through its most densely populated area. As the prevailing winds blew from the north, one could sail upstream and float downstream. Agricultural productivity was high because of the abundant and reliable flow of Nile water and the annual renewal of topsoil in the form of silt.

Egypt produced a surplus that the Pharoahs and the Ptolemies used to support a brilliant civilization. From the first to the tenth century, it was siphoned off, first to Rome and then to Constantinople. After the Muslim conquest, it was redirected to Damascus and then to Baghdad. Under the Fatimid, Ayyubid, and Mamluk regimes, tribute ceased, but in 1516, Egypt became a provincial backwater under a Turkish viceroy, paying tribute to the Ottoman sultan. Foreign rule generally impeded trade through the Red Sea to the Indian Ocean, which had flourished in the first and second centuries and was restored from the tenth to the fifteenth century. Virtually all trade with Europe disappeared from the fourth until the twelfth century. The entrepôt trade, manufactured exports, and population of Alexandria withered away. In 1820, Egyptian population and per capita income were below their eleventh-century level.

The Maghreb

In West Africa, Roman ships did not venture beyond Cape Bojador (just south of the Canary Islands), because the prevailing winds made it impossible for them to make the return journey. Overland trade between the western provinces of Africa and the lands to the south was negligible. Roman settlement was essentially coastal except in Tunisia, where large irrigated estates were worked mainly by tenant farmers. Exports of these provinces were heavily concentrated on grain shipped to Italy from Carthage and olive oil from Tripolitania. Roman economic activity in Morocco was vestigial.

When the Arabs conquered the Maghreb, they severed the Mediterranean trading links that had previously existed and explored new opportunities across the desert. They established camel caravan routes from Tunisia and Libya deep into the Sahara to places where it was possible to trade horses for black slaves. Bigger profits could be derived from the gold trade with ancient Ghana (about 800 kilometers northwest of modern Ghana, between the Senegal and Niger rivers, just inside the southern boundary of modern Mauritania), which had a lengthy history as a state before the Arabs established contact in the early eighth century. The most direct route was through Morocco, the area that received the greatest stimulus from the new contacts with black

Africa. Muslim merchants on these new routes were active in making converts to Islam. Early in the eleventh century, ancient Ghana was the first of the black African states to convert to Islam.

Gold production increased steadily in West Africa from the eighth century onward (see table 11). Until the twelfth century, most of the output circulated within the Muslim world, but from then onward there was increasing demand from Europe, mainly from Genoa, Venice, Pisa, Florence, and Marseilles. European traders conducted their operations in Muslim ports on the Mediterranean coast. They had no direct contact with African gold-producing areas until the second half of the fifteenth century, when Portugal gained access to the West African coast.

From the eighth to the twelfth century, the main market for Muslim traders was Awdaghast in Ghana. The goldfield was at Bambuk, somewhat farther south, but its exact location was kept secret. Most exports were in the form of gold dust, which was melted and molded into ingots. In the fourteenth century, the pressure of demand was such that production was started farther south at the Akan mines (in present-day Ghana). In the fifteenth and sixteenth centuries the main trading center for gold was Timbuktu in the empire of Songhai. Mining wealth was the main reason why ancient Ghana, Mali, and Songhai were able to emerge as powerful states. Income from gold produced an economic surplus that allowed the rulers to maintain the attributes of power. It made it possible for them to import horses and weapons and maintain cavalry forces.

The main barter transactions between the Maghreb and black Africa were exchange of salt for gold. In the Sahel region, salt was very scarce but was a necessity for people doing heavy work. Some of the salt came from maritime sources on the Atlantic coast. But it was much easier to transport rock salt. From the eleventh to the sixteenth century, the main source of salt was in the Sahara at Taghaza, where it was mined by slaves, cut into large blocks, and transported south by camel. Salt was not the only trade item in this north-south trade. There was also a lively exchange between trading centers within the Sahel and West Africa, particularly in kola

TABLE 11

GOLD OUTPUT: WORLD AND MAJOR REGIONS, 1493–1925
(million fine ounces)

	1493–1600	1601–1700	1701–1800	1801–1850	1851–1900	1901–1925
Africa	8.153	6.430	5.466	2.025	23.810	202.210
Americas	8.976	19.043	52.014	22.623	140.047	152.463
Europe	4.758	3.215	3.480	6.034	17.379	8.296
Asia			0.085	6.855	49.150	51.900
Australasia					104.859	62.658
Other	1.080	0.161	0.161	0.498	0.986	
World Total	22.968	28.849	61.206	38.036	336.231	477.527

SOURCE: Ridgway (1929, 6).

nuts, the African equivalent of coffee or tobacco. Farther east, Kanem was the main center of the slave trade. At a later stage, there was a diversity of gold routes to Morocco, Algeria, Tunisia, and Egypt and from Mediterranean ports to European customers. In the eleventh and twelfth centuries, Muslim countries were the only ones to mint gold coins. Marseilles first issued them in 1227, Florence in 1252, and Venice in 1284.

Black Africa

In spite of the advance beyond hunter-gatherer techniques, the agriculture of black Africa contrasted sharply with that of Egypt. There was an abundance of land in relation to population, but soils were poor and not regenerated by manure, crop rotation, or natural or human provision of irrigation. Consequently, there was extensive shifting cultivation, with land being left fallow for a decade or more after the first planting. Nomadic pastoralists were generally transhumant over wide areas for the same reason: poor soils. The main agricultural implements were digging sticks, iron hoes for tillage, and axes and machetes for clearing trees and bush.

There were no ploughs (except in Ethiopia) and virtually no use of traction animals in agriculture. There were no wheeled vehicles, watermills, windmills, or other instruments of water management.

There were no individual property rights in land. Tribes, kin-groups, or other communities had customary rights to farm or graze in the areas where they lived, but collective property rights and boundaries were vague. Chiefs and rulers did not collect rents, land taxes, or feudal levies. Their main instrument of exploitation was slavery. Slaves were generally acquired by raids on neighboring groups. Hence, there was a substantial beggar-your-neighbor element in intergroup relations.

It is not clear how widespread slavery was before contact with Muslim Africa, but the contact certainly reinforced the institution, because it made it possible to derive a substantial income from export of slaves across the Sahara (see table 12). The traffic was organized by Muslim traders from the North. The flow from north to south was negligible. Slaves usually walked through the desert with a caravan of camels carrying food, water, slave drivers, and other passengers.

Transport facilities in black Africa were poor. Camels thrived in the dry heat of the desert but could not function farther south. Muslim Africa had ships that could navigate and trade in the Mediterranean, and in Egypt there was substantial and relatively safe travel on the sailing boats of the Nile. In the Sahel and West Africa, there were partially navigable rivers, particularly the Niger, the Senegal, and Gambia, but most river traffic moved in primitive paddleboats made of hollowed-out tree trunks, and the frequency of cataracts meant that merchandise frequently had to be trans-shipped by head porterage. Horses were very expensive and had a short life expectancy because of the climate and their high sensitivity to tsetse flies. They were used almost exclusively for military and prestige purposes by the ruling groups.

A striking feature of black Africa before contact with the Islamic world was universal illiteracy and the absence of written languages (except in Ethiopia). This made it difficult to transmit knowledge across generations and between African societies. Contact with

TABLE 12

SLAVE EXPORTS FROM BLACK AFRICA, 650–1900, BY DESTINATION
(thousands)

	650–1500	1500–1800	1800–1900	650–1900
Americas	81	7,766	3,314	11,159
Trans-Sahara	4,270	1,950	1,200	7,420
Asia	2,200	1,000	934	4,134
Total	6,551	10,716	5,448	22,713

Source: Maddison (2003a, 194).

Islam brought obvious advantages. The Arabs who came as traders had a written language and an evangelizing bent. They included sophisticated members of the Muslim intelligentsia (ulama), who were able to promote knowledge of property institutions, law, and techniques of governance. Before the Moroccan conquest of Songhai in 1591, Muslim visitors were generally peaceful and posed no threat to African chiefs and rulers. The chiefs saw clear advantages in Islamization, which helped them build bigger empires and acquire stronger instruments of coercion. They were able to exchange gold and slaves for horses and weapons (steel sword blades and tips for spears and, at a later stage, guns and gunpowder). Black African traders also saw the advantages of conversion. As converts (dyulas), they became members of an ecumene with free access to markets well beyond their previous horizons. Thus, there was a gradual spread of hybrid Islam in black Africa from the eleventh century onward. Conversion had its main effect on the ruling groups, whose insignia and sanctions of power were a mix of Islam and tradition, while most of their subjects continued to be animists.

Analysts of state formation in black Africa make a distinction between complex and acephalous groups (see Goody 1971). There was a great variety of polities within black Africa. The differentiation grew wider as a result of the varying degree of contact with Islam. Slave traders were generally the most Islamized. Slaves tended to be taken from the acephalous, stateless, and least-Islamized groups. There were two reasons for this. The Muslim states tended to have the most powerful armed forces, and they generally avoided enslaving Muslims.

The European Encounter with Africa

Until the fifteenth century, European commercial contact with Africa was confined to purchases of Asian spices in Alexandria and gold on the Tunisian coast.

Portugal attacked Morocco in 1415 with the intent to conquer and get direct access to African gold. It captured Ceuta and, by 1521, had established several bases on its Atlantic coast, but Moroccan forces recaptured these in 1541 and in 1578 annihilated a Portu-guese invasion force. However, Portuguese innovations in the design of ships and navigational instruments made it possible to circumnavigate Africa and trade directly with India and other Asian destinations from 1497 onward.

The Portuguese created a trading base at Arquim on the Mauretanian coast in 1445, where cloth, horses, trinkets, and salt were exchanged for gold. In 1482, a strongly fortified base was created at Elmina, on the coast of present-day Ghana, which gave better access to the Ashanti gold mines. They succeeded in diverting a substantial part of West African gold exports from the Maghreb and got smaller amounts in East Africa from Mutapa in northern Zimbabwe. The Portuguese discovered quickly that the disease environment in sub-Saharan Africa was very hostile to European settlement. It was, in fact, the reverse of the situation in the Americas: Europeans had very high mortality from African diseases, but Africans were not particularly susceptible to European diseases.

Portugal created an island settlement at São Tomé (in the Bight of Guinea), where sugar production was developed with slave labor. The Portuguese also acted as intermediaries in the slave trade, buying and selling in African coastal markets. With the discovery of the Americas, it became more profitable and healthier for Europeans to expand sugar production in Brazil than in Africa. Portugal became the major slave trader across the Atlantic.

Although the Portuguese pioneered the export of African slaves for plantation agriculture in the Americas, they did not invent African slavery. Between 650 and 1500, 6.5 million slaves had been shipped from black Africa across the Sahara to Arabia, the Persian Gulf, and India. However, the Atlantic trade led to a massive increase in enslavement.

Over the course of the seventeenth century, Portuguese slaving activity in Africa met fierce competition from the Dutch, British, and French. The British exported more than 2.5 million slaves, most of them from Sierra Leone and the Guinea coast. The French took 1.2 million from the Senegal-Gambia region and the Dutch about half a million, mainly from the Gold Coast. The Portuguese were driven out of these regions and concentrated on shipments from Angola to Brazil and Spanish America. The Portuguese shipped about 4.5 million slaves from 1500 to 1870.

In the majority of cases, African traders controlled the slaves until the moment of sale. They brought them to the coast or the riverbanks, where they were sold to European traders. Within Africa, slaves were acquired in several ways. Some were the offspring of slaves. A large proportion were captured in wars or supplied as tribute by subject or dependent tribes. Criminals of various kinds were a steady source. There was large-scale raiding of poorly armed tribes without strong central authorities and kidnapping of individual victims.

The flow across the Atlantic rose from an average of 9,000 slaves a year in 1662–80 to a peak of 76,000 in 1760–89. Lovejoy (2000) shows the average price per slave in constant (1601) prices for 1663–1775. In 1663–82, the average price was £2.9, and £15.4 in 1733–75. African income from slavery therefore appears to have risen more than fortyfold from the end of the seventeenth to the end of the eighteenth century. At its peak, in the late eighteenth century, Klein (1999, 125) suggests that it probably represented less than 5 percent of West African income.

The demographic losses were concentrated in the tribes and people least able to protect themselves. Population growth in black Africa was certainly reduced by slave exports. Between 1500 and 1820, the population grew about 0.15 percent a year compared with 0.26 in

Western Europe and 0.29 in Asia. The disruption caused by slavery reduced income in the areas from which slaves were seized. The trade goods slave exporters received in exchange raised consumption but had little impact on production potential. In the eighteenth century, these goods included Indian textiles made specially for the West African market, tobacco and alcohol, jewelry, bar iron, weapons, gunpowder, and cowrie shells from the Maldives.

Slavery within black Africa rose substantially after the abolition movement reduced the Atlantic flow and the price of slaves dropped. The momentum of enslavement continued, and a much larger proportion of the captives were absorbed within Africa. Lovejoy (2000, 191–210) estimates that, at the end of the nineteenth century, 30–50 percent of the population of the western, central, and Nilotic Sudan were slaves. In the 1850s, half the people in the caliphate of Sokoto in northern Nigeria were slaves. In Zanzibar, the slave population rose from 15,000 in 1818 to 100,000 in the 1860s. There was a large increase of slave employment in peasant and plantation agriculture, producing palm oil products, peanuts, cloves, and cotton for export. In the Belgian Congo and Southeast and South Africa, there was a rapid expansion of mining activity at the end of the century, with a servile labor force whose de facto situation was equivalent to slavery.

An important result of Portuguese contact with black Africa was the introduction of crops from the Americas. The most important were roots and tubers. Cassava (manioc) was brought from Brazil to the Congo, the Niger delta, and the Bight of Benin early in the sixteenth century. It had high yields and was rich in starch, calcium, iron, and vitamin C. It was a perennial plant, tolerant of a wide variety of soils, invulnerable to locusts, drought resistant, and easy to cultivate. It could be left in reserve, unharvested, for long periods in good condition after ripening. Cassava flour could be made into cakes for long-distance travel and was a staple food for slaves in transit across the Atlantic. Maize was introduced in Senegal, the Congo basin, South Africa, and Zanzibar. Sweet potatoes were another significant addition to Africa's food supply and capacity to expand population.

Over the centuries, these crops were widely diffused. In the mid-1960s, three-quarters (43 million tons) of the African output of roots and tubers came from cassava and sweet potatoes (see United Nations Food and Agriculture Organization 1966). Maize (15 million tons) represented a third of black Africa's cereal output; the traditional millet and sorghum, 47 percent; rice, 12 percent; and other cereals, 8 percent. Other significant American plants were beans, peanuts, tobacco, and cocoa. Bananas and plantains were Asian crops widely diffused in East Africa before the Portuguese arrived. Coffee, tea, rubber, and cloves were later introductions from Asia.

European countries did nothing to transmit technical knowledge to Africa, nor did they attempt to promote education, printing, and development of alphabets. China had printing in the ninth century, Western Europe from 1453, Mexico in 1539, Peru 1584, the North American colonies from the beginning of the seventeenth century, and Brazil in 1808. The first printing press in Africa was established in Cairo in 1822.

In 1820, there were only 50,000 people of European descent in Africa (half of them at the Cape), compared to 13.4 million in the Americas. As noted, Africa had diseases that caused very high rates of mortality to Europeans, though Africans were not particularly susceptible to European diseases. Africans had much better weapons with which to defend themselves than the indigenous population of the Americas. The situation changed in the nineteenth century. Due to improvements in European weaponry, transport (steamboats and railways), and medicine (quinine), the number of people of European origin in Africa rose to 2.5 million in 1913.

We should note some African institutions that hindered development, but were not due to European influence. Writing toward the end of the fourteenth century, Ibn Khaldun commented at length on the fragility of the states that emerged in the Muslim world (a point that applies a fortiori to black Africa). He demonstrated the persistence of tribal affiliations and lineages and the continuance of nomadic traditions destructive of attempts to develop sedentary agriculture and urban civilization. He stressed the cyclical rise and fall of

Muslim regimes and saw no evidence of progress since the seventh century.

African societies failed to secure property rights. The power elite were autocratic and predatory, which inhibited accumulation of capital and willingness to take business risks. This was very obvious in the Mamluk regime in Egypt. There were few countervailing forces in African societies that could challenge the power elite. Goitein's (1967–93) detailed scrutiny of the Cairo Geniza archive led him to be very upbeat about the emergence in the eleventh century of a commercial business class in Fatimid Egypt, but freedom of enterprise was snuffed out in later dynasties. The most striking example of deficient property rights was slavery itself, which was closely linked with the polygamous family structure and limitations on the rights of women. These two institutions were probably the major impediment to physical and human capital formation.

Notes

1. This view has had various advocates since Arnold Toynbee first popularized the industrial revolution metaphor in 1884. Recent devotees include the neo-Malthusian Le Roy Ladurie (1966, 1978), who considered the French economy stagnant from 1300 to 1720, and the deeper pessimism of Phelps Brown and Hopkins (1981), whose real-wage approach suggested that English living standards in 1800 were well below their level in 1264 and 60 percent lower than in 1500. The most recent and sophisticated analysis in this tradition is that of Joel Mokyr (2002). He provides a detailed, erudite, illuminating, but complex history of the interaction of propositional and prescriptive (useful) knowledge since the mid-eighteenth century, with a more cursory acknowledgment of what happened earlier. He suggests (pp. 31–32) that "most techniques before 1800 emerged as a result of chance discoveries, trial and error." He makes a grudging acknowledgment of the importance of printing (p. 8) and only a fleeting reference to advances in shipping and navigation technology but is dismissive about their impact, arguing that "these earlier mini-industrial revolutions had always petered out before their effects could launch the economies into sustainable growth. Before the Industrial Revolution, the economy was subject to negative feedback; each episode of growth ran into some obstruction or resistance that put an end to it. . . . The best known of these negative feedback mechanisms are Malthusian traps, in which rising income creates population growth and pressure on fixed natural resources." He is very insistent on the narrowness of the "epistemic base" before 1800 and argues that positive feedbacks between the two types of knowledge have increased hugely in the course of three industrial revolutions since the eighteenth century. There was a cascading interaction (p. 100), and we have now arrived at a point where modern information technology has produced "an immensely powerful positive feedback effect from prescriptive to propositional knowledge" (p. 115). His analysis

of the economic impact of knowledge is based on assertions rather than quantitative evidence. These are presented with characteristic fervor; for example, take his assessment of the impact of his second industrial revolution: "The pivotal breakthrough in the propositional knowledge set was the identification of the structure of the benzene molecule by the German chemist August von Kekulé in 1865. . . . The discovery of the chemical structure is a paradigmatic example of a broadening of the epistemic base of an existing technique" (p. 85). My problem with Mokyr's analysis is with his judgment on the impact of science and not with his model, which can be useful in explaining why the scientific revolution of the seventeenth century had a delayed payoff and why the innovative impact of science and technology accelerated in the past two centuries. The problem is that he assumes no net improvement in living standards before 1800 and a constantly accelerating cornucopia since then. This contradicts the quantitative findings of historical national accounts in the Kuznetsian tradition for the period before and after 1800 (see tables 1–4). Mokyr is of course aware of this. In his defense (pp. 116–17), he suggests that "aggregate output figures and their analysis in terms of productivity growth may be of limited use in understanding economic growth over long periods. The full economic impact of some of the most significant inventions over the past two centuries would be entirely missed in that way." Instead he opts for the Silicon Valley serendipity of Bradford DeLong (2000). DeLong's hallucinogenic approach to economic history is derived from that of Nordhaus (1997).

2. The main advocates of this view are Paul Bairoch (1981), Fernand Braudel (1984), Andre Gunder Frank (1998), and Kenneth Pomeranz (2000), all of whom asserted that China was ahead of Europe until 1800. The first two changed their opinion. Pomeranz presented the most elaborate analysis of the nature and timing of the "great divergence" between China and Western Europe. He suggested that Western Europe was "a none-too-unusual economy: it became a fortunate freak only when unexpected and significant discontinuities in the late eighteenth and especially nineteenth centuries enabled it to break through the fundamental constraints of energy and resource availability that had previously limited everyone's horizons" (p. 207). I have explained my disagreement with Pomeranz at length in Maddison (2003a, 248–51).

3. Tables 1–7, 9, and 10 and my figures give a summary quantitative picture of developments in the world economy and major regions over the past millennium. The methodology of my macromeasurement, with

country and intertemporal detail, can be found in Maddison (2003a) and on my website (2003b). Modern standardized accounts provide a coherent macroeconomic framework covering the whole economy, cross-checked in three ways. From the income side, the accounts are the total of wages, rents, and profits. On the demand side, they are the sum of final expenditures by consumers, investors, and government. From the production side, they are the sum of value added in different sectors—agriculture, industry, and services—net of duplication. The framework can be expanded to include measures of labor input and capital stock, labor, and total factor productivity. Macromeasurement in these three dimensions and rudimentary growth accounts originated in the seventeenth century with the work of William Petty (1623–87) and Gregory King (1648–1712). In the twentieth century, there has been an enormous extension in the coverage of official national accounts. Their international comparability has been greatly enhanced in two ways: (a) by the creation of standardized guidelines (the latest version is the *System of National Accounts*, 1993, published jointly by the EU, IMF, OECD, UN, and World Bank; these agencies have played an active role in helping national statistical offices to conform to the standardized system); and (b) by the development of purchasing power parities (PPPs) to convert the gross domestic product (GDP) estimates of different countries into a common unit. PPP converters provide a much better basis for estimating relative levels of output and expenditure than exchange rates. PPP-adjusted estimates in 1990 prices are available for 2001 for 99.6 percent of world GDP.

The temporal scope of real GDP estimates has been enormously expanded by the efforts of quantitative economic historians, inspired in large part by the work of Simon Kuznets (1901–85). He was mainly interested in "modern economic growth" from 1760 onward, which he contrasted with an earlier period of "merchant capitalism" from the end of the fifteenth to the second half of the eighteenth century. The evidence now available suggests that the acceleration in West European growth took place around 1820 rather than 1760 and has modified the old emphasis on British exceptionalism. In the past thirty years, there has been a rapid expansion in studies of long-term growth in Asia and Africa, so that coverage of economic growth worldwide is much more satisfactory than in Kuznets's day.

Demographic material can also be important in providing clues and cross-checks on estimates of per capita income in the distant past. One striking example is the urbanization ratio. Thanks to the work of de Vries

(1984) and of Rozman (1973), one can measure the proportion of the population living in towns with more than 10,000 inhabitants in Western Europe, China, and Japan. In the year 1000, the urbanization ratio was zero in Europe (only four towns had more than 10,000 inhabitants), and in China it was 3 percent. By 1800, the West European urban ratio was 10.6 percent; the Chinese, 3.8 percent; and the Japanese, 12.3 percent. When countries expanded their urban ratio, one can assume that there was a growing surplus beyond subsistence in agriculture and that the nonagricultural component of economic activity was increasing (see Maddison 1998). The Chinese bureaucracy kept population registers that go back more than 2,000 years. These bureaucratic records were used to assess taxable capacity, and they include information on cultivated area and crop production, which was used by Perkins (1969) to assess long-run movements in Chinese GDP per capita.

4. There is considerable disagreement on the size of the preconquest population of the Americas. The two extreme protagonists are Rosenblat and Borah. Angel Rosenblat (1945) suggested a total of 13.4 million, relying to a considerable extent on literary evidence at the time of the conquest. Woodrow Borah (1976, p. 17) suggested a total "upwards of 100 million." His aggregate estimate was derived mainly by extrapolation, "admittedly hasty and general," of his results for central Mexico where he compared his 25 million estimate for preconquest Mexico with 1 million in the Spanish census of 1605 and assumed a depopulation rate of 95 percent. The evidence for his 25 million figure is flimsy. If such a level had been attained by 1500, it is highly unlikely that it would have taken 400 years for Mexico to recover. In Europe, it took only 150 years to regain the population level before the Black Death, with much less technical advance than occurred in Mexico. My estimate for the population of the Americas in 1500 is about 20 million (see Maddison 2001, 231, 233–36 for the derivation of this figure, and Maddison 1995b for a much more detailed analysis of Mexico).

5. *Encomienda, repartimiento, mita,* and debt peonage were variant ways of mobilizing indigenous labor in Spanish colonies, some of which had roots in precolonial practice. In the Viceroyalty of Peru, the *mita* system involved compulsory labor; virtually all labor in the silver mines was of this kind. In Mexico, the Aztec tax system involved levies in kind, which could be commuted by supplying labor. The initial Spanish practice was to allot these levies in a given area to Spaniards who had helped in the conquest or otherwise gained official favor. Some of these *encomiendas*

were hereditary, but many were not. Over time, most of these claims were forfeited, and with the growing monetization of the economy, taxes were levied in silver or commuted in the form of labor. Thus, there was a growth of "free" labor in Mexico, but those who could not meet the tax obligation were ensnared in various forms of debt peonage. As the indigenous population had the legal status of children, there was obviously a large element of coercion. In this situation, it is not surprising that slavery remained unimportant in Mexico. The northern parts of the Viceroyalty of New Spain were inhabited by Chichimecs and other hunter-gatherer groups who could not be tamed and found it easy to avoid capture once they acquired horses. See Macleod (1984) for a detailed analysis of these variants.

6. Initially, Spain (or rather the kingdom of Castile) divided the Americas into two administrative units: the viceroyalties of New Spain and Peru, with their capitals in Mexico City and Lima, respectively. The former included or came to include present-day Mexico, the Caribbean, Central America (Guatemala, Honduras, Belize, Nicaragua, and San Salvador) and part of what is now the United States (California, Colorado, Florida, Louisiana, Nevada, New Mexico, Texas, and Utah). The Viceroyalty of Peru included the rest of the Americas from Panama to the south, with the exception of Brazil, whose western boundary was fixed by the Treaty of Tordesillas in 1494. The viceroyalties were divided into thirty-five governorships at one time or another in the sixteenth and seventeenth centuries. The Philippines, whose conquest was begun in 1567, was a governorship dependent on New Spain. A separate Viceroyalty of New Granada was created in 1739, with its capital at Bogotá. It included present-day Colombia, Ecuador, Panama, and Venezuela. In 1776, another viceroyalty, Rio de la Plata, was created, with its capital at Buenos Aires. It included Argentina, Bolivia, Chile, Paraguay, and Uruguay. In 1750, the Treaty of Madrid modified the Tordesillas boundary of Brazil, enlarging threefold the area recognized as Portuguese (see Brading 1984 on the nature and impact of the eighteenth-century administrative changes).

7. The Dutch made early and ambitious attempts to create an empire in the Americas. Their first ventures occurred during the Spanish occupation of Portugal, which cut off access to their traditional salt supply in Setúbal. From 1599 to the 1620s, they developed an alternative source in salt pans at Punta de Araya on the coast of Venezuela. They created the Dutch West India Company to harass Spanish shipping, participate in the slave trade, and engage in sugar production. Between 1630 and 1654,

they occupied the northeast coast of Brazil (Recife and Paraíba), where sugar plantations and export trade were developed by sephardic Jewish settlers from Amsterdam (mainly of Portuguese origin). Access to the slave trade was opened by the Dutch seizure of Elmina, Luanda, and twenty other Portuguese outposts on the African coast. The profitability of slavery and sugar was buttressed by the rapid expansion of sugar refining in Amsterdam. In 1654, the Dutch were expelled from Brazil and moved their sugar activity farther north. Plantations were developed in Suriname and the area that became British Guiana in 1803 (Demerara, Essequibo, and Bernice). They also initiated and financed sugar production in Barbados and Martinique but, in the 1660s, were expelled by the British and French. They continued to operate as slave traders and merchants from island bases in Curaçao (which they acquired in 1637), St. Eustatius, and St. Martin and remained as relatively marginal sugar producers in Suriname. The Dutch colony of New Netherlands, with its capital New Amsterdam, had been taken over by the British in 1664. In 1674, it was formally ceded (as New York) in exchange for a free hand in Suriname.

References and Recommended Reading

Bairoch, P. 1981. The Main Trends in National Economic Disparities since the Industrial Revolution. In P. Bairoch and M. Levy-Leboyer, eds., *Disparities in Economic Development since the Industrial Revolution*. London: Macmillan.

Bethell, L., ed. 1984–92. *The Cambridge History of Latin America*. 10 vols. Cambridge: Cambridge University Press.

Borah, W. C. 1976. The Historical Demography of Aboriginal and Colonial America: An Attempt at Perspective. In W. M. Denevan, ed., *The Native Population of the Americas in 1492*, 13–34. Madison: University of Wisconsin Press.

Brading, D. A. 1984. Bourbon Spain and Its American Empire. In L. Bethell, ed., *The Cambridge History of Latin America*. Vol. 1, 389–439. Cambridge: Cambridge University Press.

Braudel, F. 1984. *The Perspective of the World*. London: Fontana.

Bray, F. 1984. Agriculture. In J. Needham, ed., *Science and Civilisation in China*. Vol. 6, 2. Cambridge: Cambridge University Press.

Bresnahan, T., and R. Gordon, eds. 1997. *The Economics of New Goods*. Chicago: University of Chicago Press.

Clark, C. 1940. *The Conditions of Economic Progress*. London: Macmillan.

Crosby, A.W. 1972. *The Columbian Exchange: Biological and Cultural Consequences of 1492*. Westport, Conn.: Greenwood Press.

DeLong, B. 1998. Estimating World GDP, One Million B.C.–Present. Available at www.j-bradford-delong.net.

———. 2000. Cornucopia: The Pace of Economic Growth in the Twentieth Century. Working Paper 7602. Cambridge, Mass.: National Bureau of Economic Research.

De Vries, J. 1984. *European Urbanization, 1500–1800*. London: Methuen.

Eisenstein, E. L. 1993. *The Printing Revolution in Early Modern Europe*. Cambridge: Cambridge University Press.

Eisner, G. 1961. *Jamaica, 1830–1930: A Study in Economic Growth*. Manchester, U.K.: Manchester University Press.

Engerman, S. L., and B. W. Higman. 1997. The Demographic Structure of the Caribbean Slave Societies in the Eighteenth and Nineteenth Centuries. In F. W. Knight, ed., *General History of the Caribbean*. Vol. 3, 45–104. London: UNESCO.

EU, IMF, OECD, UN, and World Bank. 1993. *System of National Accounts*. Brussels: EU, IMF, OECD, UN, and World Bank.

Frank, A. G. 1998. *Reorient: Global Economy in the Asian Age*. Berkeley and Los Angeles: University of California Press.

Galileo, G. 1632. *Dialogue on the Great World Systems*. With annotations and introduction by G. de Santillana. Chicago: University of Chicago Press, 1953.

Gilbert, M., and I. B. Kravis. 1954. *An International Comparison of National Products and Purchasing Power of Currencies*. Paris: OEEC.

Goitein, S. D. F. 1967–93. *A Mediterranean Society: The Jewish Communities of the Arab World as Portrayed in the Documents of the Cairo Geniza*. 6 volumes. Berkeley and Los Angeles: University of California Press.

Goodman, D., and C. A. Russell. 1991. *The Rise of Scientific Europe, 1500–1800*. London: Hodder and Stoughton.

Goody, J. 1971. *Technology, Tradition and the State in Africa*. Oxford: Oxford University Press.

———. 1983. The Development of the Family and Marriage in Europe. Cambridge: Cambridge University Press.

Grassman, S., and E. Lundberg, eds. 1981. *The World Economic Order: Past and Prospects*. London: Macmillan.

Habib, I. 1978. The Technology and Economy of Moghul India. *Indian Economic and Social History Review* 17, no. 1:1–34.

Higman, B. W. 1984. *Slave Populations of the British Caribbean, 1807–1834*. Baltimore: Johns Hopkins University Press.

Ho, P. T. 1959. *Studies on the Population of China, 1368–1953*. Cambridge, Mass.: Harvard University Press.

International Energy Agency. 2004a. *Energy Balances of OECD Countries 2000–2001.* Paris: OECD.

————. 2004b. *Energy Balances of Non-OECD Countries 2000–2001.* Paris: OECD.

Khaldun, Ibn. 1958. *The Muqaddimah: An Introduction to History.* 3 vols. Trans. Franz Rosenthal. London: Routledge and Kegan Paul.

Klein, H. S. 1999. *The Atlantic Slave Trade.* Cambridge: Cambridge University Press.

Kravis, I. B., A. Heston, and R. Summers. 1982. *World Product and Income: International Comparisons of Real Gross Product.* Baltimore: Johns Hopkins University Press.

Kuznets, S. 1953. *Economic Change: Selected Essays.* New York: Norton.

————. 1966. *Modern Economic Growth.* New Haven, Conn.: Yale University Press.

————. 1973. *Population, Capital and Growth: Selected Essays.* New York: Norton.

Lal, D. 2001. *Unintended Consequences.* Cambridge, Mass.: MIT Press.

Landes, D. S. 1965. Technological Change and Development in Western Europe, 1750–1914. In H. J. Habakkuk and M. Postan, eds., *The Cambridge Economic History of Europe.* Vol 6, part 2. Cambridge: Cambridge University Press.

————. 1969. *The Unbound Prometheus.* Cambridge: Cambridge University Press.

————. 1998. *The Wealth and Poverty of Nations.* London: Little, Brown.

Le Roy Ladurie, E. 1966. *Les paysans de Languedoc.* Paris: Mouton.

————. 1978. *Le territoire de l'historien.* Vol. 2. Paris: Gallimard.

Lebergott, S. 1984. *The Americans: An Economic Record.* New York: Norton.

Lewis, W. A. 1981. The Rate of Growth of World Trade, 1830–1973. In S. Grassman and E. Lundberg, eds., *The World Economic Order: Past and Prospects.* Cambridge: Cambridge University Press.

Lin, J. Y. 1995. The Needham Puzzle. *Economic Development and Cultural Change* (January): 269–92.

Lovejoy, P. E. 2000. *Transformations in Slavery.* Cambridge: Cambridge University Press.

Macleod, M. J. 1984. Aspects of the Internal Economy of Colonial Spanish America: Labour, Taxation, Distribution and Exchange. In L. Bethell, ed.,

The Cambridge History of Latin America. Vol. 2. Cambridge: Cambridge University Press.

MacPike, E. F. 1932. *Correspondence and Papers of Edmond Halley.* Oxford: Oxford University Press.

Maddison, A. 1971. *Class Structure and Economic Growth: India and Pakistan since the Moghuls.* London: Allen and Unwin; New York: Norton.

—. 1982. *Phases of Capitalist Development.* Oxford: Oxford University Press.

—. 1987. Growth and Slowdown in Advanced Capitalist Countries: Techniques of Quantitative Assessment. *Journal of Economic Literature* 25, no. 2 (June): 649–98.

—. 1995a. *Monitoring the World Economy, 1820–1992.* Paris: OECD.

—. 1995b. *Explaining the Economic Performance of Nations: Essays in Time and Space.* Aldershot, U.K.: Elgar.

—. 1998. *Chinese Economic Performance in the Long Run.* Paris: OECD.

—. 2001. *The World Economy: A Millennial Perspective.* Paris: OECD.

—. 2003a. *The World Economy: Historical Statistics.* Paris: OECD.

—. 2003b. Website. Available at http://www.eco.rug.nl/~Maddison/.

—., and B. van Ark. 2000. The International Comparison of Real Product and Productivity. In A. Maddison, D. S. Prasada Rao, and W. Shepherd, eds. *The Asian Economies in the Twentieth Century.* Aldershot, U.K.: Elgar.

McEvedy, C., and R. Jones. 1978. *Atlas of World Population History.* Middlesex, U.K.: Penguin.

McNeill, J. R., and W. M. McNeill. 2003. *The Human Web: A Bird's-Eye View of World History.* New York: Norton.

Mitchell, B. R. 1975. *European Historical Statistics.* London: Macmillan.

Mokyr, J. 2002. *The Gifts of Athena: Historical Origins of the Knowledge Economy.* Princeton, N.J.: Princeton University Press.

Morineau, M. 1985. *Incroyables gazettes et fabuleux métaux.* Cambridge: Cambridge University Press.

Needham, J. 1970. *Clerks and Craftsmen in China and the West.* Cambridge: Cambridge University Press.

—. 1981. *Science in Traditional China: A Comparative Perspective.* Cambridge, Mass.: Harvard University Press.

Nordhaus, W. 1997. Do Real Wages and Output Series Capture Reality? The History of Lighting Suggests Not. In T. Bresnahan and R. Gordon, eds., *The Economics of New Goods.* Chicago: University of Chicago Press.

O'Rourke, K. H., and J. G. Williamson. 2002. After Columbus: Explaining Europe's Overseas Trade Boom, 1500–1800. *Journal of Economic History* 62, no. 2 (June): 417–56.

Perkins, D. W. 1969. *Agricultural Development in China, 1368–1968.* Chicago: Aldine.

Phelps Brown, H., and S. V. Hopkins. 1981. *A Perspective on Wages and Prices.* London: Methuen.

Pomeranz, K. 2000. *The Great Divergence: China, Europe and the Making of the Modern World Economy.* Princeton, N.J.: Princeton University Press.

Prakash, O. 1998. *European Commercial Enterprise in Pre-Colonial India.* Cambridge: Cambridge University Press.

Qaisar, A. J. 1982. *The Indian Response to European Technology and Culture.* Bombay: Oxford University Press.

Ridgway, R. H. 1929. *Summarized Data of Gold Production.* Economic Paper No. 6. Washington, D.C.: Bureau of Mines, U.S. Department of Commerce.

Rosenblat, A. 1945. *La Población Indígena de América desde 1492 hasta la Actualidad.* Buenos Aires: ICE.

Rozenzweig, F. 1963. La economía Novo-Hispaña al comenzar del siglo XIX. *Revista de Sciencias Políticas y Sociales,* UNAM (July–September).

Rozman, G. 1973. *Urban Networks in Ch'ing China and Tokugawa Japan.* Princeton, N.J.: Princeton University Press.

Shepherd, V., and H. M. Beckles, eds. 2000. *Caribbean Slavery in the Atlantic World.* Princeton, N.J.: Wiener.

Smil, V. 1994. *Energy in World History.* Boulder, Colo.; Oxford, England: Westview Press.

Smith, A. 1776. *An Inquiry into the Nature and Causes of the Wealth of Nations.* Reprint. Chicago: University of Chicago Press, 1977.

Solow, B. L., ed. 1991. *Slavery and the Rise of the Atlantic System.* Cambridge: Cambridge University Press.

Teng, S. Y., and J. K. Fairbank. 1954. *China's Response to the West: A Documentary Survey.* Cambridge, Mass.: Harvard University Press.

Thomas, R. P. 1965. A Quantitative Approach to the Study of the Effects of British Imperial Policy upon Colonial Welfare: Some Preliminary Findings. *Journal of Economic History* 25, no. 4 (December): 637.

Toynbee, A. 1884. *Lectures on the Industrial Revolution in England.* London: Rivingtons.

United Nations Food and Agriculture Origanization. 1996. *FAO Production Yearbook.* Rome: FAO.

Usher, A. P. 1932. Spanish Ships and Shipping in the Sixteenth and Seventeenth Century. In *Facts and Figures in Economic History.* Festschrift for E. F. Gay. Cambridge, Mass.: Harvard University Press.

Williams, E. 1970. *From Columbus to Castro: The History of the Caribbean, 1492–1969.* London: Deutsch.

Woytinsky, W. S., and E. S. Woytinsky. 1953. *World Population and Production: Trends and Outlook.* New York: Twentieth Century Fund.

About the Author

Angus Maddison, a British economist and economic historian, is an emeritus professor of economics at the University of Groningen in the Netherlands. His work focuses on assessing the forces affecting national and global economic growth, with a particular emphasis on quantitative analysis in a historical and comparative perspective. Educated at Cambridge, McGill, and Johns Hopkins universities, Maddison has been an economic advisor to the governments of Brazil, Ghana, Greece, Mexico, and Pakistan and has held senior positions at the Organisation for Economic Co-operation and Development. He is the author of numerous works on long-term economic growth, most recently *The World Economy: Historical Statistics* (OECD, 2003).